THE CHRIST
OF EVERY ROAD

THE CHRIST
OF EVERY ROAD

DR. RICHARD LINDE

Pleasant Word
A Division of WINEPRESS PUBLISHING

Packaged by Pleasant Word, PO Box 428, Enumclaw, WA 98022. The views expressed or implied in this work do not necessarily reflect those of Pleasant Word. The author(s) is ultimately responsible for the design, content and editorial accuracy of this work.

Unless otherwise noted, all Scriptures are taken from the Holy Bible, New International Version, Copyright © 1973, 1978, 1984 by the International Bible Society. Used by permission of Zondervan Publishing House. The "NIV" and "New International Version" trademarks are registered in the United States Patent and Trademark Office by International Bible Society.

Scripture references marked KJV are taken from the King James Version of the Bible.

Scripture references marked NASB are taken from the New American Standard Bible, © 1960, 1963, 1968, 1971, 1972, 1973, 1975, 1977 by The Lockman Foundation. Used by permission.

ISBN 1-4141-0298-4
Library of Congress Catalog Card Number: 2004097307

This book is for Laraine Linde, my friend and companion of many years, a historian and a scholar in her own right, who had the forbearance not to intrude, but to believe in my writing.

I also am grateful for a supportive family and the comments of friends new and old; for a varied education and the multiple jobs necessary to pay for it; and for the opportunity to study other cultures while making travel films.

Most of all, I am thankful for the words of my sources: Matthew, Mark, Luke, and John.

The cover photo was taken by the author in the front range of the Rockies in Colorado.

Richard Linde

THE QUEST OF THE HISTORICAL JESUS

He comes to us as one unknown,
    without a name,
        as of old,
            by the lakeside,
    he came to those who knew him not.

He speaks to us, he speaks the same word:
    "Follow thou me!"
        and sets us to the tasks
            which he has to fulfill
                for our own time.

He commands, and to those who obey,
    whether they be wise or simple,
        he will reveal himself
            in the toils,
                the conflicts,
                    and the sufferings
    which they shall pass through
    in his fellowship.

And as an ineffable mystery,
    they shall learn in their own experience
        who he is.

by Albert Schweitzer

Table of Contents

CHAPTER 1

Sauntering on the Fast Track

Jesus Said, "I Am the Way . . ."

Life on the fast track:

> run,
> > run,
> > > run,
> > > > run,
> > > > > run.

On the weekends, clean up the yard, relax, have a party. Then back on the fast track:

> stress,
> > stress,
> > > stress.

But shouldn't we saunter once in awhile? You know, stroll, or just walk a little?

Of course, some would insist, "If I did that, I'd get run over! Why, in the 20th century alone, we introduced power airplanes, computers, air conditioning, the internet, and rockets to outer space, not to mention TVs, FMs, VCRs, and CDs—more new technology than had come along in two millennia!"

Isn't that all the more reason to saunter, though? We'd have more time to think WHERE we are going, or WHY, because technology by itself cannot move us forward. Aldous Huxley suggests, for instance, that some of our technological progress "allows the world to move backward more rapidly."

For those of us on the fast track, consider this:

1.

First, we need homes, not just houses.

Today tremendous advances have been made in architecture. The designs of today are not just fads. The past half century has brought a revolution in building because of structural glass, steel, pre-stressed concrete, solar heating, and cantilever design. The schools of architecture today are not even teaching many of the older patterns.

No longer will the person doing the laundry rub-a-dub-dub the clothes over a corrugated washboard at the cost of skinned knuckles and an aching back. We just drop the soiled clothes into a gleaming white washer, set the dials and the machine blasts off!

How did the mother of a large family a few generations ago get her work done, before electricity, steam irons, and deep freezers—before automobiles, supermarkets, frozen foods, and shopping centers? Perhaps she did not.

We have escalators, air conditioning, and amazing audio systems, and we are not sure any more whether God did all this or whether it was strictly ourselves.

One little boy became lost in a department store. His mother went to the office, and they said they could page him over the P.A. system, which would be heard all over the store. The boy heard his name all right and was suitably impressed. He replied, "Yes, God, I'm right here!"

Today undoubtedly we are more comfortable. We do have more efficient houses. But the question is this: Do we have better homes? Study the divorce statistics. Better homes? If our houses are more livable, why do we spend so little time in them?

One challenge those on the fast track today should hear is this: Instead of thinking of the houses we would like to build, perhaps we should give more attention to the homes we are making. We need the Carpenter of Nazareth to make homes out of houses.

2.

Next, as we tear along on the fast track, our race must be for wisdom, not just knowledge. Knowledge is simply the gathering of information. Wisdom means using that information for the best life.

It was the last minutes of the football game, and the team was three points behind and 82 yards from the goal line. The quarterback told the team to tighten up; they were going to win the game. So he called a play to the right and gained 12 yards. He then called a play to the left that gave them another 10 yards. Then several more plays, and they worked again and again. The stands were bedlam, and the team was on the half-yard line.

Then, of all things, the quarterback called a very complicated double reverse to the right. The coach was screaming but the team did not hear him and they made a touchdown. After it was all over and the team was celebrating in the locker room, the coach cornered the quarterback and asked, "Why, why, why did you call that last play? It was much too complicated! Why not a simple quarterback sneak?"

"Well," the quarterback replied, "number six to the right and number seven to the left were working so well, I just decided to add up number six and number seven and I got 14, so I called 14 to the right."

"You fool," the coach said. "Six and seven do not add up to 14. Six and seven are 13!"

"Well, coach, if I'd been as smart as you are, we'd have lost the game."

You see, knowledge is not necessarily wisdom. There is no question that we know more today than any people in history. Many schoolboys and girls today have more information than geniuses of past centuries. We have knowledge, but we need wisdom.

How do you solve the desegregation problem? How do you stop war? How do you distribute America's amazing food supply to starving people of the world and still pay a just price to the farmer? How do you give something to a needy person and not make him or her feel like a beggar? Sometimes we know all the answers, except the important ones.

We need wisdom, not just knowledge.

3.

Also, I would like to suggest to all of us on the fast track that we try the Great Physician, Jesus, not just drugs and medicines.

What do you suppose is the major public health problem in the United States today? Aids? Smoking? Cancer? Heart disease? No, not any of those.

According to Dr. Elizabeth McSherry, writing in the *Harding Journal of Religion and Psychiatry*, volume III, number I, "The major United States public health problem . . . is lack of spiritual identity formation." In other words, she says that ABSENCE OF SPIRITUAL LIFE is the major public health disorder.

Dr. McSherry says this primary spiritual disorder has many secondary disorders, such as teen suicide, that has tripled over the last 15 years and is now the leading killer of white males, age 15–24. She also cites teen pregnancies, homicides, addiction, and adult lifestyle problems. These secondary disorders originate in the human spirit, she states. Many professionals who deal with chemical dependency agree. For years they have considered chemical addiction to be a spiritual disorder.

One thing that bothers me most about our civilization is we often expect health to be done FOR us, rather than BY us. "I'm nervous this afternoon. Isn't there something I can take for it?" "Oh, I've had a rough day. I need a drink."

It was Carl Jung, the late, great Swiss psychiatrist, who said, "Most of my patients don't need me. They need God."

4.

Next, as we rocket along through life, we need direction, not just speed.

It was not so many years ago that my grandfather hitched two horses, Roxie and Pet, to his wagon and drove 17 miles from Sycamore Valley in Ohio to Woodsfield and back. It took all day!

Awhile ago, I left Tel Aviv, Israel, on Saturday at noon and came halfway around the world and preached a sermon the next morning in my church in the USA.

Speed.

I suppose my grandchildren will spend their vacations in the Craters of the Moon National Park, not the one in Idaho but on the moon itself!

We have speed, but we need direction. In Peter Marshall's phrase, "We are saving more time, but we aren't putting the time we save to any better use. We have better ways of getting places, but no better places to go."

Not long ago, a person would miss a stagecoach, shrug his shoulders, and say, "Oh, well, there'll be another one along in a day or two." Today, we go shopping and curse if we miss one section of a revolving door.

An American was visiting missionary friends in the interior of Africa. They lived in a village on the edge of the jungle, and one morning he decided to peer into the dense foliage.

He soon was absorbed with what he was seeing: ferns as high as trees formed a canopy above him, palms like umbrellas in the sky, rare plants he had never seen before, and exotic tropical birds. Eventually, he decided to retrace his steps but soon realized he had gone too far into the jungle and was lost.

He walked desperately in what he thought was the right direction, but the jungle became more and more dense. Soon he was wandering aimlessly.

Finally, he came to a clearing with a few grass and mud huts. He found a native and asked if he could get him out. The native said he could.

"All right," the man said. "Show me the way."

"Walk," the native said. So they walked and hacked their way through unmarked jungle for more than an hour. The man became worried.

"Are you sure this is the way? Where is the path?"

"Bwana," he said, "in this place there is no path. I am the way."

- - - - - - - - -

Centuries ago, Jesus also said those words, as reported by John, "I am the way . . . the truth . . . the life."

###

CHAPTER 2

Hey, It's Jesus!

THE UNCOMMON POWER OF JESUS

A few nights ago I could not sleep, so I got up and roamed around the house. Then I turned on the TV. The only thing I could find was an old Italian film entitled *La Dolca Vita*. The opening scene of the movie shows a helicopter flying through the sky, not very high above the ground. Hanging down from the helicopter is a large statue of a man dressed in robes with his arms outstretched. He appears almost as though he is flying.

The helicopter flies over farmland, where some men are working. They see the helicopter and wave. Then one of them recognizes who the statue is and shouts in Italian, "Hey, it's Jesus!" They run after the helicopter and laugh and call to the statue.

Before long the helicopter reaches the outskirts of Rome, where it passes over a swimming pool, which is surrounded by some girls in bikinis, basking in the sun. The helicopter stops to hover over the pool, and the girls start waving. The men in the copter try to get the girls' telephone numbers over the noise of the engine.

Fred Buechner, the author and storyteller, writes that he once saw this movie in a college town theatre crowded with students and their dates. He said there was a kind of snickering all through the theatre at the absurdity of the sacred statue hanging in the sky and the Italian young men trying to get acquainted with the girls. When the copter continues on its way, for the first time, the camera starts to zoom in on the statue with the arms outstretched, and the screen is almost filled with the face of Jesus. He said that the snickering and conversation stopped abruptly.

I began to wonder why—why on a date night in a theatre did the attention focus on the screen rather than on each other. What force or spirit or magnetic power is in the story of Jesus today?

Remember it all started out well. We have the beautiful story of a baby born in a manger, with shepherds and angels and sheep all mixed up together, and finally the Magi coming from the East to present gifts to Jesus. But that is not the whole story! After the Wise Men arrived, an angel appeared to Joseph and said, "Rise, take the child and his mother and flee to Egypt, and remain there until I tell you, for Herod is about to search for the child to destroy him."

Now, it so happened that the Magi, on their way to see the Christ child, had stopped to get directions from King Herod, since they were kings themselves. They asked, "Where is he who has been born king of the Jews?" That disturbed Herod considerably, because he himself was the king, and he did not want any competition. So, according to Matthew, "Herod, in a furious rage, sent and killed all the male children in Bethlehem and in all that region who were two years old or under." Jesus had escaped, of course, with Mary and Joseph to Egypt, after being warned by an angel.

We should not be surprised that King Herod could do such a thing, though, for he was a master of assassination. Earlier he had killed the members of the Sanhedrin, the Supreme Court of the Jews, and slaughtered 300 court officers. He murdered his wife, Miriamne; her mother, Alexandra; and three of his own sons. One writer of the time said, "It is safer to be Herod's pig, than his son."

When Herod had ordered the slaughter of the infants, he killed perhaps twenty or thirty, but not hundreds, because Bethlehem was not a large town. Today archaeologists have uncovered a slit trench under the Church of the Nativity in Bethlehem in which were buried a number of young male babies at about the time Jesus was born. Today if you visit Manger Square in Bethlehem and enter the Church of the Nativity, you can see the skeletons of these babies, which scholars think could very well be the actual boys killed by Herod.

The question arises, though, WHY COULDN'T THE GOSPEL WRITERS HAVE LEFT THAT OUT, when they told the story of that first Christmas? Why not leave the story with the fuzzy sheep and the dignified kings coming into the stable area of an inn, where dogs were barking and chickens were cackling? Why not stop with the birth and forget the grim details?

The reason they included that part of the story is that it would not have been accurate without it. It would not have been a life story to which everyone, everywhere could relate.

This is a story of GOD TRYING TO TELL US WHAT HE IS LIKE. It is a drama of power: The power of God and the power of people clashing in a stable.

Did you ever stop to think how many kinds of power there are? Beauty is a form of power. Love is power. Truth is power. Military force is power. A child in a supermarket wanting candy, and when he is refused, he lies down in the supermarket aisle and has a tantrum—that, too, is power.

Back when Stalin was dictator of Russia, he was told that the Pope opposed the mass slaughter of the Kulaks. Stalin laughed and asked, "How many battalions does the Pope have?" Obviously, Stalin never had thought of power other than military might. Napoleon also was a man of force, and he, too, said that God was on the side of the strongest battalions.

After he was exiled to the island of St. Helena, Napoleon reversed himself. He said, "Caesar, Alexander, Charlemagne and I have founded empires. We founded them on force, and they are gone. Jesus alone founded his empire on love, and at this hour millions of people would die for him whom they have never seen."

Many years ago, Canon Streeter defined power as the ability to accomplish purpose. Power is not power, he said, unless it accomplishes what it is trying to do. An ax, for instance, is good for chopping wood but not for shaving. Dynamite is powerful for demolishing old buildings but not for lulling a baby to sleep. Nuclear power can create all kinds of good energy, but we are afraid of it because it can be misused. Nuclear power is not very effective in clearing the world of hate.

When our oldest son, Rick, was in high school, I was trying to get him to do something he did not want to do. I do not even remember what it was. Perhaps I thought he should wear his hair longer or shorter than it was—something world shattering like that. I do remember, though, there was loud talking and arguing. A few days later, I happened to look in his room, and I saw a sign I had never noticed before. It said, "There is no power like the power of gentleness."

There are different kinds of power, you see. There is the power of Big Government or the power of the Mafia or the power of a child throwing a tantrum. But there also is the power of beauty and the power of truth and the power of devotion.

It is strange that nations or civilizations seldom are defeated by external forces. First they go to pieces by weakness within. Someone said that the Roman Empire fell 400 years before anybody knew it. A hundred years before Christ, the Chinese built a Great Wall to keep out the enemy. It was invulnerable.

At intervals all along the length of the Great Wall were lookout towers and at every gate a garrison of soldiers.

The nation was invaded three times, but the enemy did not breech the walls or fight the soldiers. They simply bribed the gatekeepers and marched in. As a Chinese Christian leader once said, "It is easier to fight the bandits in the hills, than to fight the bandits in our hearts."

Dostoyevsky, the great Russian writer, knew about it. In 1862 he wrote a novel entitled *The Possessed*. It was a story of corruption in old Russia before the Communist revolution broke.

One of his characters says this, "We'll start an upheaval. There's going to be such an upset as the world has never seen. Listen, I know who's on our side: a teacher who laughs at God is on our side, judges who take bribes, juries who acquit criminals, schoolboys who murder peasants for the sake of a thrill are ours . . . . Already the Russian God has been vanquished by cheap vodka. The peasants are drunk, the mothers are drunk, and the churches are empty. This generation has only to grow up."

When Jesus told his disciples how his kingdom would come on earth, he said it would be like light and salt or seeds growing. This is the power of Jesus. It is not the power of kings, despots, or tyrants. It is not even the power of bosses. It is uncommon power. Like yeast, his spirit would permeate the minds of people. That is how ideas come.

Galileo Galilei had an idea. He amassed evidence that proved the earth revolved around the sun and is not the center of the universe, as had been believed. Now we all think that idea.

We think the thoughts of Shakespeare. More recently Martin Luther King said something about civil rights, and today millions believe it. We listen to the musical thoughts of the Beatles or Elvis or Beethoven or Mozart.

Jesus began with a dozen men, not exactly brilliant persons. He would have been glad to have better. As someone wrote,

"They were slow to understand what he said, even slower to grasp what he was . . . . He was in their homes where people laughed, he was where they fished and traded and swore and prayed, all so ordinary." Yet, little by little the spell of his mind was on their minds.

In our day, the spell of Jesus' mind was on Bob Ziemer. He wanted to translate the New Testament into the Vietnamese language. Bob Ziemer was my college roommate. He had a facility for languages and studied college Greek, which I thoroughly detested.

After finishing his studies, he became a missionary and later was assigned with his wife to a mission station in the highlands of South Vietnam, about 170 miles northeast of Saigon.

Eventually Bob was the first person to translate the New Testament into the Vietnamese language.

Then tragedy struck.

The Viet Cong overran the village and killed six of the missionaries, including Bob Ziemer. Two others were believed to be captured. Bob's wife, who was pregnant at the time, was wounded but managed to escape and send the story back to America by radio telephone.

I can remember Bob's earnestness, his dedication, and the long hours he spent preparing for his work. One church official said of the six who were killed, "I feel certain that, even if they had known their fate, they would not hesitate to go in again."

I am sure this was true with Bob. He would much rather be on the firing line with Jesus Christ than doing anything else with his life. Bob had an idea.

And what happened to Bob's wife and the child with whom she was pregnant when Bob was killed? She now is retired and living in Florida, and the son she was carrying has become an Admiral in the United States Navy.

God, too, had an idea. "God loved the world so much that he gave his Son, his only Son . . ." That is the story of the first

Christmas. It is a drama of power, God's power and man's power. God is saying, "I'll not use my power. I'll put myself in your power. I'll become a little child."

So that first Christmas, God walked down the stairway of heaven to a world of kings and killings, to a stable in Bethlehem . . . with a baby in his arms.

###

CHAPTER 3

What Jesus Is Really All About

THE POWER TO TURN ON YOUR LIFE

Jesus came to bring us good news. Good News! The Good News is that God is not a far-off tyrant whose major desire is that we obey all kinds of minor regulations. God is here, a friend who wants the best for us!

Jesus came to lead us away from petulant, petty, and pinched ways of living. "I came that they might have life," Jesus said, "and have it abundantly (John 10:10)."

A man named Jesse Cotherman took his nine-year-old son to the local billiards parlor. This was an introduction to a whole new world, since the boy had never touched a cue, let alone smashed a rack of balls. First dad showed him how to grip the cue, then how to make a bridge, and finally how to strike the ball just the right way to give it spin. Then dad sat on a nearby stool and said, "Play."

Of course, the boy was everywhere, bouncing the ball off the table, scraping the cue on the felt. He even managed to smack the rack man's thumb. Meanwhile his dad sat watching and smiling but rarely giving advice. After an hour he called it quits and took the boy home.

A week passed, and one morning as Jesse, who was the man telling the story, was heading for work, his wife pressed a crumpled note into his hand. "Read it when you get to the office," she said. "It'll make your day." Dad could not wait. As soon as he was out of the driveway, he fumbled for the paper. He pulled over to the curb and spread it out on the steering wheel. It was his son's handwriting, and the boy scrawled, "My dad's the best. He loves me even when I scratch."

It was now nearly forty years later, and the man reached into his coat pocket and pulled out a yellowed piece of paper. "That was years ago, but I still carry my son's old note, 'He loves me even when I scratch.'" That is the Good News. That is life.

There was a Roman soldier who came to Julius Caesar with a request for permission to commit suicide and end his life. He was wretched and miserable. Caesar looked at him and said, "Man, were you ever really alive?" A surplus of life, a super-abundance. Life.

Jesus was telling about the Good Shepherd, but the people who were listening did not understand what he meant. In typical fashion, instead of getting into complicated explanations, Jesus told them another story. It was about two kinds of sheepfolds of that day. In the villages and towns, there were communal sheepfolds where all the village flocks were sheltered at night when they returned home. These folds were protected by a strong door, for which the guardian of the door had the only key.

In the warm season, when the sheep were out on the hills, they did not return to the village at night. Instead they were collected into sheepfolds on the hillside, which were just flat places enclosed by a wall with an opening through which the sheep entered and departed. There was no door, so the shepherd himself would lie down across the opening. The sheep could not get out, nor could thieves or marauding wild beasts enter, except over his body. The shepherd was the door.

Certainly this was in Jesus' thoughts when he said, "I am the good shepherd . . . . I am the door" through which people can find a loving God. Until then many thought of God as a stranger or even as an enemy. Thieves and robbers would come and steal or even destroy the sheep. Jesus had a totally new mission, which he described with some of the most explosive words he ever uttered. He said, "I came that they might have life, and have it abundantly." Abundant life—that is what Jesus really is all about!

In the middle 1800s, Ralph Waldo Emerson, one of America's greatest essayists and philosophers, was getting close. He said there is something that he called "The Oversoul." The Oversoul empowers those who know how to tap into it to do things they normally cannot do. Emerson describes the experience:

It can help poets write more sublimely,
thinkers to think more boldly,
runners to run more swiftly,
teachers to teach more inspiredly,
doctors to bring healing more effectively.

There is a report with the title, *There's More to Life Than Not Being Sick.* It contains a national study taken among physicians who are general practitioners. They say that illness is about 90% spiritual and 10% bio-physical. If they had the power to remove every sign of disease and could diagnose every pathology and treat it, there still would be problems because LIFE IS MORE THAN NOT BEING SICK. Ninety percent have no medically treatable symptoms, this study says, but the people are *genuinely sick.* They are not hypochondriacs, they are not malingerers, but if these people do not get help somewhere, they WILL become physically sick. What this report is saying is that we must understand the spiritual nature of people.

This is the message of the Bible. In the Old Testament, the word was "shalom." When a Jew meets another Jew, he or she says, "shalom." Commonly we think of shalom as meaning "peace," which it does, but it also means much more. It means everything God meant us to be: physically, mentally, spiritually, and emotionally. Totally. "Have it all, brother. Shalom, sister, have it all."

Of course, being humans, we could not leave something so simple and grand alone. We had to make all kinds of interpretations, rules, and regulations. Religion told people when they could and could not reap wheat, certainly not on the Sabbath, when they could and could not look at a woman, when they could go to the movies, when they could play cards, when they could put out a fire—again, not on the Sabbath. Jesus had to tell us all over that we became too tangled up in rules and regulations, as other religions do. "What I'm offering," said Jesus, "is different. I came that you might have life and have it abundantly."

Years ago I studied Greek. I hated every minute of it, but I did learn something. For instance, I learned the Greek word Jesus used in the story of the Good Shepherd, as quoted earlier from the Gospel of John, is "zo-ay," translated "life." Life pressed down, heaped up, and running over. "Zoay, that's why I came," said Jesus. "I came that you might have life," the life God intended, a quality of life, and an intensity. It is love, joy, peace, and power. It is everything God means us to be. "Total life—that's why I came," said Jesus.

You see, the Bible is not a theological, head-trip book. It is a clinical book, an experience. It is about what happened to this good king or that bad one. It is about the Israelites who sometimes loved God and sometimes did not. It is about ordinary people whose names we still remember, who served God sometimes poorly but other times in extraordinary ways.

There is a man named Keith Miller who was in the oil business. He is a layperson, not a minister, and he had an experience that changed him. He says:

> I had a wife whom I loved very much and two babies I loved deeply, but there didn't seem to be any purpose to my life. One day as I was driving through the tall pine woods country of East Texas I suddenly pulled up beside the road and stopped. I remember sitting there in complete despair. I had always been an optimistic person, and usually thought that after a good sleep or perhaps a couple martinis I could start over again tomorrow. But now it seemed like I was on a great gray treadmill going no place, in a world that was made of black clouds.
>
> As I sat there I looked up toward the sky and said. "If there's anything you want in this stinking soul, take it." That was almost ten years ago, but something came into my life that day which has never left. There wasn't any ringing of bells or flashing of lights or visions, but it was a deep intuitive realization of what it is God wants from a man, which I have never known before. And the peace which came with this understanding, seemed like the conflict of a lifetime had ceased. I knew to the core of my soul that I have somehow made personal contact with the very meaning of life.

That sort of thing was happening constantly in the ministry of Jesus. He found his world full of unpromising people—prodigal sons, Samaritan women at the well, dishonest public servants like Zacchaeus, and fishermen like Peter, James, and John. They were getting nowhere with their lives, and he left them with a new vision and hope.

The great psychologist and Harvard professor, William James, called that process "conversion," which he said is "the process, gradual or sudden, by which a person hitherto consciously wrong and unhappy, becomes consciously right and happy." Other scientists today have gone further, believing that God can indwell the part of the brain (cerebral cortex), that brings us to a higher spiritual level where impossible things become possible.

"I came that you might have life and have it abundantly," said Jesus.

There was an interview in *Time Magazine* with Aleksandr Solzhenitzyn, possibly the most distinguished Russian writer of his day. He had been branded a traitor to the Russian state and was sent to a prison camp in the dreaded gulag of Siberia. He wrote that there was an elderly man who came in completely exhausted at the end of their tortuous workday and threw himself on his bunk just above Solzhenitzyn's. Then he would reach under his blanket and pull out some words scribbled on worn scraps of paper that turned out to be words copied from the Bible, from the Gospels. Read in such grizzly circumstances, these words transformed the old man into a brotherly, loving fellow human being. God was not a theory but a presence.

In another place, a minister was telling about his own personal experience. "James was my playmate," he said, "and he changed my life. He lived with Miss Hacker as her foster child four doors down on the other side of the street. In the backyard, there were a couple old cars, and in our imaginations we went on trips around the country." James was exceptional, though, because he was always happy. He was bright enough in school, but his real gift was for living. He was even a good loser, and he loved Jesus Christ almost as if he were a playmate. The minister said he went to church for the first time at James' invitation.

When James was 17, a virus no larger that the point of a pin entered his body. His large, muscular frame was attacked overnight by forces neither of them could understand. Suddenly James was on crutches and then bedridden. Everything he had hoped for seemed smashed, yet he laughed. "Look at me. Who would have thought I'd be a cripple!"

For two years, the boy visited his friend. Slowly James fought back and regained the use of his limbs. Sometimes James even cheered up his visitor and sent him away glad to be alive. James at last decided to be a minister and talked about the day when he would have a church of his own and lead his own youth group. He talked about his goals, his happiness, and his mission. Finally his legs were strong enough to take a job as a dishwasher to earn enough money for school.

"He worked for three weeks and three days," the minister said. The next morning, in front of the restaurant where he worked, he stepped off the bus on his crutches and was killed instantly by a passing car. "James was my first friend and now, thirty years later, I often think of him," the minister said. "I never dreamed of being a minister before he died. Now, for half my life, I have been what he wanted to be."

James was an orphan, he was poor, and he was often teased because of his clumsiness. He was smashed by a dreaded disease, and finally he was dead at 21. "And yet, to this day," the minister said, "I have never known a happier person. He was honest, he was loving, and he was caring."

And so it is. Jesus came to give us health, joy, faith, caring—zoay, shalom. "I am come," said Jesus, "that you might have life . . . life . . . life."

###

CHAPTER 4

On Earth, Who Prevails?

THE POWER TO BE MEEK

In the newspapers recently, there was a story about a man who was so weak he could not resist assisting his domineering lover in murdering her husband. He was described as a "meek little murderer."

Meekness: spinelessness, submissiveness, and ineffectiveness. We say a person is "as meek as a mouse," shy, frightened, trying to get out of the way. Mice are not particularly attractive, and neither are the meek. Is it not true that many of us are convinced that if a person is going to get anyplace in this world, he or she has to push to get there" We may not be aggressive, but it is okay to be "assertive," the new word.

Then we hear of Jesus going to the mountain and sitting down and teaching the people, "Blessed are the poor in spirit, for theirs is the kingdom of heaven. Blessed are those who mourn, for they shall be comforted." Then he says something that has always startled me, "Blessed are the meek, for they shall inherit"—not the great beyond, not some never-never land off in the future someplace, but—"Blessed are the meek for they shall inherit THE EARTH!"

We admire strength, don't we? We teach our children to stand up for themselves. We object to this Beatitude because WE JUST DO NOT BELIEVE THE MEEK WILL INHERIT THE EARTH! They may get to heaven and be happy there, but they cannot expect very much in THIS world. And yet, it is in THIS world where Jesus says the meek get their reward.

Perhaps the greatest mistake we make when we think of this Beatitude of Jesus is that we confuse meekness with weakness. In my early ministry, there was a preacher who was unusually talented. He was determined, too, to be what we call a "success." He became embroiled in the politics of the church and, of course, was always friendly with people who could help him. He did not have much time for the others. One day he said to me, "Why do you waste your time on those guys? They can't do anything for you." That attitude began a process of moral decay in this minister, and eventually his whole career collapsed.

By comparison, let me tell you about Frank Laubach. Laubach is dead now, but not long ago, he was known all over the world as "the Apostle of Literacy." In the early 1940s, he founded the organization which became known as "Laubach Literacy International," and the organization went into 100 different countries teaching people to read in 300 languages.

Frank Laubach started out as a missionary in the Philippines and while there wanted very much to be chosen president of the Theological Seminary in Manila. Laubach had the qualifications: he was a brilliant teacher, an able administrator, and he also thought he had the votes of the trustees.

Now, there is nothing wrong with wanting to be president of a theological seminary. Laubach thought he could make it, until the votes were counted, and he was one vote shy. One trustee whom he thought was his friend voted against him. This cost him the presidency of the seminary. As a result, Laubach became bitterly resentful, so much that his work and health began to fail because of his brooding. Almost in desperation he turned to God.

That sounds strange to say about a man who already was a missionary, but there are some uncommitted missionaries, teachers, and preachers. Then Laubach, without reservation, committed his life to God, and from that hour he had only one desire: to do what God wanted him to do.

To prove to himself that he actually had made a complete commitment, Laubach went to another island in the Philippines, where there could be no possible hope of church preferment. The island was Mindanao. There Laubach lived among the Moros, who at that time were still headhunters.

For many months, Laubach lived in the greatest danger among them. The Moros were fierce, and no missionary had been able to touch them. Eventually he won their confidence, and finally began Christian work among them. In the years since then, the whole world has honored Frank Laubach, but his real work began among the headhunting Moros of Mindanao. A friend of his described this experience by saying, " . . . Out of that beginning, came a reborn, meek, God-controlled Frank Laubach."

Two ministers, both ambitious, both wanting to be used, but WHO INHERITS THE EARTH?

Let's discuss that word "meek" for a moment, because there really is no English word that accurately expresses the meaning. The Hebrew word for meek means "being molded." In other words, the meek are the "God molded" in the Old Testament. Think of Moses, for instance. He is the one character in the Bible, other than Jesus, whom the scripture specifically calls meek.

Of course, Moses was no weak, anemic creature. Moses was a man of such fiery passions that in his youth he killed an Egyptian in a fit of anger. After he led the Israelites out of their slavery in Egypt, he listened to their complaining, time after time after time. They did not like the food, and one time there was an insurrection led by several of Moses' friends and relatives.

They did not like the water either. Moses tried to get water out of a rock that he struck again and again in a fit of anger. For that little display, God said Moses would not be the one to lead the people of Israel into their Promised Land. Eventually, though, the scripture would say about Moses that he was "very meek, above all the men on the face of the earth."

Meekness is not weakness. Meekness is power blended with gentleness.

When the New Testament states this Beatitude, the Greek word for meekness is "praos," and praos suggests the taming of wild animals. One night my wife, Randy, and I stayed in Cody, Wyoming, on the ranch of Bill Cody, the grandson of "Buffalo Bill" Cody. Randy and I had just unpacked our bags when we heard a real ruckus up the valley, and we went there to investigate. Several of the cowhands had brought in some wild ponies from the back pasture of the ranch. The ponies were there in the corral and had to be broken. They were lassoed, and much against their will, they were bridled and saddled.

One of the cowhands was an excellent rider. He mounted the pony, and even in rodeos, I have never seen such bucking, snorting, and kicking. The cowhand held his mount, and after several rides around the corral, the pony was tamed, under control, and now ready for his owner, Bill Cody, to put him to work.

Now, that is EXACTLY THE WORD THE NEW TESTAMENT HAS FOR MEEK. They are God-tamed! Think of Saul of Tarsus, who later became Paul, the Apostle. He was rushing around Palestine like a wild animal, raging against this new Christian sect. He was fairly snorting in his anger! Then one day on the road to Damascus, Saul was corralled by God and thrown to the ground. He heard a voice saying, "Saul, Saul, why do you persecute me . . . . It's hard for you to kick against the ox goad." That was the beginning of Saul's taming. He became meek, in the sense of being God tamed.

Meekness is power blended with gentleness.

It is interesting to notice the French version of the Beatitude. While the English version says, "Blessed are the meek," the French version says, "Blessed are the debonair." The spiritless characters we usually call "meek" certainly are not "debonair." Carefree, lighthearted, debonair. There is logic to the French version: the meek are God's gentlepersons, God trained, above pettiness, not burdened with grudges. "Blessed are the debonair."

A leading businessman uses this prayer everyday as he begins work at his desk: "God, this business belongs to you. Though I am president of this corporation, I am working for you. May your spirit guide me and direct me this day in my decisions and my relationships . . . . May what is done in this organization be pleasing to you. Amen." Blessed are the God-tamed, the God-molded.

In that sense, is it true that the meek gain the earth? Jack Nicklaus said he never could become a winner in golf until he learned to control his temper. In education, no one can teach the person who knows it all already. So the meek inherit . . .

Charles Rann Kennedy wrote a drama entitled *The Terrible Meek*. It is set in first century Palestine in the time of Jesus. In it a Roman centurion says, "We go on building our kingdoms, the kingdoms of this world. We stretch out our hands, greedy, grasping, tyrannical, to possess the earth. Domination, power, glory, money, luxury, these are the things we aim at. But what we really gain is pestilence and famine, death breathing ghosts that haunt our lives forever . . . . Possess the earth? We never did possess it. We have lost both the earth and ourselves in trying to possess it."

In the climactic scene of *The Terrible Meek* where Jesus is being crucified, the centurion stands in the shadow of the cross and says to Mary, "I tell you, woman, this dead son of yours, disfigured, shamed, spat upon, has built a kingdom this day that can never die . . . . The earth is his . . . . Something happened up here on this hill today to shake all kingdoms of blood and fear to the dust . . . . The meek, the terrible meek are about to enter into their inheritance."

"Blessed are the meek," said Jesus. "THEY inherit the earth."

###

CHAPTER 5

Are You Afraid of Being Too Good?

BEING DECENT IN AN INDECENT WORLD

Over Memorial Day weekend in the spring, a church in Ohio has a Family Life Conference every year. It has become a tradition for the younger families to participate, and there are special activities for groups of all ages. One year a man from denominational headquarters in New York was the adult speaker and discussion leader. His name was Bill Elliott—DOCTOR Bill Elliott, no less. Bill had not just one but two PhDs. Bill also had some unusual, even far out ideas, and after awhile we began calling him "Wild Bill" Elliott.

Perhaps his most unusual idea was expressed one morning toward the end of the conference, when someone asked what his greatest desire or goal was in life.

Bill said, "I think my greatest desire in life is to be a saint."

There was stunned silence. A young woman asked, "A what?"

Bill repeated, "I think my greatest desire in life is to be a saint." A saint? Well, no one wants to be a saint today. Whenever anyone does anything worthwhile today, it is prefaced by saying, "Of course, I'm no saint." We are very defensive about that. There are many who want to be good people, but we do not want to go too far with it.

There is solid reason for this feeling. For a long time, so many "good" people were just plain bores, the kind of people you ducked when you saw them coming, "the noble order of mote removers and neighbor judgers." Yet, with all our rebellion against the pious masks and hypocrisy, we have not done much better than our parents did in achieving a just society.

Over a century ago in Boston, Horace Mann believed crime could be practically eliminated in this country by an increase in the size and number of our tax supported schools. We have built tax supported schools beyond anything Horace Mann dreamed. Yet, add up all we spend on education, all we spend on churches, all we spend on charity, and we are told crime in our country costs billions of dollars more than all of them combined.

Sometimes I wonder whether or not we have had a completely wrong idea about what goodness is. For a long time, we thought that a person was a Christian if he did not drink, chew, spit, play cards on Sunday, or go out with wild women. But that is not all there is to it. Remember the little girl who prayed, "O God, make all the bad people good and all the good people nice." Our goodness must be positive.

William Barclay, the great British scholar, says that the word righteousness has three meanings. It means justice, it means right living, and it means a sense of being approved by God. On the other hand, some people have the strange notion that being good involves some queer ideas demanded by God, who plays the role of a psychopathic dictator. The rules for goodness, however, are signposts set up by a friend, God, a friend who wants to keep us on the road to the fullest life.

The world we live in is built on moral foundations. The commandments of God have not been set up by God to take the fun out of life. They have been given to us to keep us from hurting ourselves. A young woman with whom I was counseling had revolted against her marriage vows, but she found that her rebellion was not so pleasant. She said, "I thought that faithful marriage wasn't much fun, but I've been living in hell since I started cheating."

The doctor will tell you that the right thing is the healthy thing. Of course it is, because that is the way the world is made. That is why worry is a sin. It gives you stomach ulcers and brings on heart attacks. That is the reason hatred and resentment are sins. They make you sick and send you to a doctor. That is why self-centeredness is a sin. It cuts you from your friends and makes you sick of yourself.

Let us take another look at that word "righteousness." It is too bad it sounds so churchy, because there is not much difference between the words righteousness and rightness. Isn't everyone looking for rightness: business people, poets, prophets, all kinds of people?

It is interesting that the words "holiness" and "health" come from the same root. Health often comes when we begin observing the laws of health: getting enough rest, eating good food in moderate amounts, exercise, and recreation. So often, though, we live our lives dominated by tension, hatred, anxiety, and fear, which Dr. Carl Jung calls "the general neurosis of our times."

Dr. Jung, you may remember, is that late great Swiss psychiatrist who wrote what many consider to be a monumental book entitled *Modern Man in Search of a Soul*. In that book, Dr. Jung says, "I have never been able to effect a lasting cure in any of my patients until the patient has discovered a living and creative faith in God." So, if you hesitate to use the word "righteous" today, try being "healthy minded," and you will come very close to Jesus' thought of righteousness. The original meaning of the word "holy," for instance, was whole, wholesome, and healthy.

Some of that came out when Jesus was teaching his Beatitudes. The fourth one says, "Blessed are those who hunger and thirst for righteousness, for they shall be satisfied."

The young people in a church I served put on a musical, a chancel drama as they called it, on Christ's Beatitudes entitled *Lightshine*. To me the most moving scene was one in which Bill Hillman came forward dressed in knickers and a ridiculous, gigantic cap, and holding a golf club. Barb Sutton was in her tennis outfit, holding a pose as she lobbed a backhand over the net, and Bob Johnson was in red Bermuda shorts, a Hawaiian print shirt, and dark glasses, carrying cameras and tons of travel posters. Then the young people sang these lines:

We have cars and boats and kids, and they're all in good condition,
That's just part of what we have because of our ambition.
We visit Spain and France and Greece, it's part of our tradition.
We have so much, that now we're bored, in spite of our position . . .
We live the good life, Lord.
O Lord, I hunger, I thirst.

I suppose we in America do not know much about hunger and thirst. However, half the people in our world today live on far less than $1,000 a year. In the ancient world in which Jesus lived, a day laborer missing one day's employment meant the rest of the family would go hungry for food.

In our modern world, or any world, there are many hungers beyond a need for food and drink. There is the hunger for rest, the hunger for play, and the hunger for sex, among others. These are called animal hungers. For instance, if we allow an animal to eat and drink its fill, to sleep when it is tired, to romp when it pleases, and to satisfy its procreative urges, the animal, if it is normal and healthy, is content.

But that is not true with people. We are animals among the animals that refuse to be satisfied by the fulfillment of animal desires. People are haunted by beyond-the-body hungers.

Many years ago, when I was a boy, I had a dog. He was a curly-haired, brown water spaniel who was afraid of the water. His name was "Pal," but while he was still a puppy making puddles in the kitchen we nicknamed him "Puddy" for obvious reasons.

Pal and I were the most intimate of friends. I shared many meals with him. I would give him some of my meat and bread, and at times I would even sneak him a bite of cake, if I could spare it. Having eaten together, we would sometimes go to the hill behind our house, and at the bottom of it, we would drink out of the same spring together (remember this was years ago before we all became so sanitary).

Now, Pal's enjoyment of eating and drinking was very keen, but having left the dinner table or the spring at the bottom of the hill, we parted company. I had hungers and thirsts to which Pal was a stranger. Sometimes in early summer, for instance, I would lie in the deep grass and watch the brook that trickled away from our little spring. Someone told me it flowed into Beaver River and that Beaver River flowed into the Mahoning River, which flowed into the Ohio River, which flowed into the Mississippi River, which then flowed into the Gulf of Mexico.

I wondered what kinds of people lived on the Gulf of Mexico, and I said to myself, "Someday I'm going to see the world. I'm going to swim in the Gulf of Mexico." And I have. But Pal never shared my dreams. He knew nothing of my eagerness to see the big world that lay beyond my private little hill. Sometimes I would read some of my homework to Pal, but he did not seem very much interested. I would even play a tune on my trumpet for him, but he did not appreciate it. In fact, he would even howl at some of the high notes.

He never cared for the colors of a sunset, and as for birds, his biggest enjoyment was chasing them rather than listening to their music. Now, Pal and I could share a hamburger or chase a baseball together, but in the higher things, we were strangers. I had a hunger that could not be satisfied with food.

People need a purpose large enough to give meaning—and pizzazz—to life. Short term purposes can keep us going for awhile. A person may like his job so well he never looks at the clock, but sooner or later, we have to look at the calendar and ask, "What's the use of it all? What's it all add up to?" We need causes that are longer and larger than our lives.

A businessman friend never took religion very seriously. He had frequent promotions and eventually was CEO of a large corporation. The higher up he moved, the emptier his life seemed. One day a young, blind employee came in for a conference, and my friend was surprised by the boy's radiance. He asked his employee what made him so happy. "Oh, I'm a Christian," he said.

After the young man left, my friend thought about the interview and compared the boy's life with his own emptiness. He prayed, and his life changed. He found peace and stability he had never known before. It is impossible, as Jesus said, for people to live by bread alone or by recognition or wealth or busyness or even self-indulgence. According to the New Testament, a Christian is a person who has come into a new relationship with God, a new quality of life.

Guiseppe had been a wealthy and respected man in pre-Mussolini Italy, but he was not enthusiastic about the new Fascist regime, because he was taxed and cheated out of his mill and vineyards. Guiseppe's nephew was a ne'er-do-well who joined the Fascists and became prominent. He liked to taunt his uncle, "See, uncle, you're not as smart as people used to say you were, nor am I as stupid. Look who's on top now."

Guiseppe bore the jibes patiently, until one day he asked, "Nephew, did I ever tell you about Morlino?"

"Morlino, who's he?"

"Morlino was once the village beggar. But he wasn't a very good beggar, because as soon as he collected a few soldi, he gambled them away on the lottery, and shortly he was poorer than ever. Then one day, fortune favored Morlino, and he won the Grand Prize. Promptly Morlino was a person of consequence in the village. He had wealth, a house, fine clothes, and everyday he would come down to the village square and throw coins to his former colleagues, the other beggars. While he was doing this, he would pass out a few words of advice. The other beggars liked the coins but didn't like the advice. Finally one beggar asked, 'What gives you the right to tell us what to do? After all, it was luck that you won the lottery!'"

"'Luck? Luck? Stupido, it was science. I figured out the winning combination. I tell you it was brains. What's a lucky number—lucky beyond any other? Seven. There are seven days in a week, the seven hills of Rome. So I took the number seven and multiplied it by itself. SEVEN TIMES SEVEN IS 56. Then I added an extra seven—567—and that was the winning number.'"

"'But seven times seven is NOT 56. It is 49!'"

"'Fool, who won the grand prize, you or I?'"

So old Guiseppe ended his story, "Yes, nephew, you are the clever one (since the year was 1939 before Mussolini was overthrown). If I had been smart enough to understand that, I, too, would have shouted 'Duce, Duce!' and I'd still have my mill and my vineyard. BUT WHAT WILL YOU SAY IF IT LATER DEVELOPS THAT SEVEN TIMES SEVEN ONCE AGAIN BECOMES 49?."

###

CHAPTER 6

Praying When You Don't Know How

THE POWER OF GOD'S PRESENCE

The disciples once asked Jesus, "Lord, teach us to pray." In that request, they were not alone. Paul did not know how to pray either. Writing to the Romans he said, "We do not know how to pray . . . but the Spirit intercedes for us with sighs too deep for words" (Romans 8:26)."

If we were honest, we, too, would admit that we do not know how to pray. We have fantasies of what we think prayer should be, images we may have picked up from grandparents who were known for their lengthy, powerful prayers. We have ideas of what we think preachers or Sunday school teachers or deacons THINK prayer should be. A lot of those ideas, though, are not much more than fantasies. They do not fit our modern age, or at least they do not fit US.

Prayer today is more than routine.

Awhile ago, there was a young woman who said she wanted to talk with me about an article by Malcolm Boyd, an Episcopal priest. "I think he has something," she began. "Here's what he says, 'The family is gathered around the dinner table. Jimmy is late, and Dad somewhat angrily declares that EVERYBODY must be present before grace can be said. Jimmy straggles in. There is a pause, and then Dad announces that it's Ann's turn. She prays:

God is great.
God is good.
and we thank Him
for our food.

Then, without taking a breath, she mutters. "Amen. Please pass the bread."

The young woman in my study continues, "That's exactly what happened in our house, so we gave up praying. Prayers like that are just routine, don't you think?" Malcolm Boyd was right. Prayer must be more than routine, or it is not a real prayer. When we use holy words in a phony manner, we teach the children that prayer is not really very important. Ann probably will not think about prayer until she becomes ill or wants to be elected Homecoming Queen. Then Ann will kind of dictate a request to God. That kind of prayer is not saying, "Thy will be done." It is really saying, "MY will be done, and I'd like to have your blessing, please."

Prayer today is more than babbling.

In the sixth chapter of the Gospel according to Matthew, the writer says. "In your prayers, don't go babbling on like the heathen, who imagine that the more they say the more likely they are to be heard." An earlier generation called prayer, "Storming the gates of heaven." There is much to be said for being earnest in our prayers, but we also must be careful not to dictate to God.

In the days of the American frontier, the people lived very close to the elements. Rain, particularly, was very important to the early settlers. Sometimes, in fact, meetings would be called just to pray for rain. Some of the prayers still survive. "Almighty

God, thou knowest how we are sufferin' down here, and we want you to come to our relief. We want you to come with no little sprinkle, but, O God in heaven, send us an old-time, old fashioned gully washer and root soaker, and be quick about it. Amen."

Prayer today is more than a proper posture. Many people seem to think that proper prayer can be made only when our hands are folded, head bowed, or even kneeling. It is interesting to note that in the record of the four Gospels, there is only one instance where Jesus kneeled to pray. When others in the Bible prayed, they were kneeling, seated, lying prostrate, walking in the fields, in prison, in bed, in the marketplace or, as Jesus prayed, even on a cross.

Prayer today is more than asking. Many never do pray, except to ask God for favors. A little boy was asked if he prayed every night, and he answered, "No, not every night, because some nights I don't want nuthin.'"

During the Civil War, Abraham Lincoln said that both the North and the South should pray, not for victory or that God should identify with one side or the other but that both the North and South should be found "on God's side."

1. PRAYER IS LISTENING

Today we live in a talking world. We spend our waking hours in a babble of tongues and voices. So much of our conversation has become not listening but waiting until we can break in to tell what WE are thinking.

I remember a conversation I had with a young woman who was a psychiatric nurse in a local hospital. She was in her late thirties, had been married for 13 years and had four children, all still at home. She was dying, she knew, of cancer, and we were talking about prayer. I asked if any of her ideas about prayer were changing.

"Oh, yes," she said. "I used to think of prayer as saying the 'right things,' being formal. But now I think of prayer as being more of a conversation with God. I'm beginning to think of prayer as listening to God, trying to learn his will for my life."

I said I liked that idea, then I asked her when she learned she had cancer.

"About two and a half years ago when I had surgery, a mastectomy. Then last October I discovered it was spreading."

"Do you remember how you felt about it?" I asked.

"Oh, I had a lot of different emotions. Sometimes conflicting emotions. There was fear, anger, depression, and a desire to fight back. Maybe even some denial. You helped me through that."

"Do you think it's the will of God for you to have cancer?"

"No I don't."

"You've prayed to be healed, haven't you?"

"Oh, yes."

"Will God answer your prayers?"

"He may or He may not, but He will help in other ways."

"Such as?"

"Learning to cope, acceptance, and having courage."

2. PRAYER IS RECEIVING

At its best, prayer is receiving, and that is hard for us. Today we make heavy demands on ourselves: action, output, and work. Tension, work, stress. Work, anxiety. But what is all our anxiety about? We say we like to be busy, and that is good.

There is an old hymn that says:

Awake, my soul
Stretch every nerve,
and press with vigor on.

We encourage that in our Christianity. We admire people of competence, aggressiveness, and action. There comes a time in our lives, though, when that is not enough. Real sorrow, for instance.

A friend had seen his five-year-old daughter killed in an accident in front of his house, and he carried her inside. What do you say to your friend? At a time like that, action, enthusiasm, or vigor are not enough.

All of us start our lives with high expectations, but we run into experiences when something deeper is needed. Serious failure, for example, and disappointment. What we had set our hearts on is gone. Beethoven, the composer, faced his loss of hearing, and his prayer was this, "O God, give me strength to conquer myself."

There are two characteristics of every strong life: action and receiving. The offices of psychiatrists are full of people who have learned the techniques of activity and aggressiveness but do not know how to receive. Prayer is receiving.

3. PRAYER ALSO IS COMPANIONSHIP

One of the most important things that can be said about prayer is that its worst perversions are associated with the idea that prayer is an emergency measure. It is more than that. Prayer is companionship with the Great God of the universe.

One minister was telling about a visit with a friend who was the father of four children. During the conversation, all four children came to him for some reason or another. The first, a small boy, came in to ask, "Daddy, may I have some money for ice cream. All the kids are going to Baskin Robbins." Later a girl of about seven came hobbling in crying. She had banged her shin while playing, and needed sympathy from her father. He kissed the wound and, amazingly, instant healing took place. The third child, a girl in her teens, came with a homework problem she could not solve, and he helped. The fourth child was the youngest and climbed up in his lap and settled down. The father asked, "What do you want, son?" The child answered, "Oh, I don't want anything. I just wanted to be with you." Prayer is companionship.

4. PRAYER IS A THOUGHT

Are you startled with that? Often we think of prayer in formal and liturgical ways:

Prayer is adoration of God. Yes, prayer is devotion to our maker, leader and friend.

Prayer is confession. Certainly! It is showing sorrow for our sins. It can be a rite, as it is in some churches, where there is private confession to a priest, then a penance and absolution for the sins.

Prayer is supplication. It is asking, sometimes urgently asking.

Prayer is thanksgiving. It is a prayer expressing gratitude. Prayer is all that. Even so, it does not need to be a ritual. It does not need to be formal. It can be a thought, a thought addressed to God.

5. PRAYER, TOO, IS DESIRE.

If I were to ask a group of people the condition of their prayer life, many would sheepishly say they do not have much. But what about your life of desire? Let us not fool ourselves by playing with words: desire is prayer. Beneath all the things we commonly call praying, what we want out of life is our prayer. Edison's search for the secret of incandescent light was his prayer. Pasteur's desire to make a discovery to help humankind was his prayer. Hitler's ambition to rule Europe was his prayer. Whatever we may have called prayer, the prayers that inevitably tend to be answered are the cravings around which our lives are organized. Desire is dangerous.

One spring I attended a reunion of my graduating class from the conservative Christian college I attended. It was interesting to see everyone again. One of my roommates had been a successful Methodist minister in Florida, but he had grown, not just portly but fat! Two other close friends seemed to have lost the spark. They were not old, but they seemed like it. A girl I had dated was still slender and pretty, and on her birthday that year, she had done a free-fall parachute jump out of an airplane.

One classmate who was not there was Burleigh Law. I remember Burleigh praying frequently for the people of Africa. If Burleigh wanted an easy life, he prayed once too often, because God sent him to Africa as a missionary. He studied agriculture, and he studied flying. The mission board sent him to Africa to teach improved methods of agriculture to the people and to fly supplies to other missionaries who were back in the bush in inaccessible places.

Then came the riots in his country, the Republic of the Congo, part of which today is called Zaire. Some of the missionaries radioed that they needed help. The situation was getting dangerous, and probably they would need to be evacuated. Burleigh said he would come for them, but they agreed that if the situation became too dangerous, they would wave him off as he flew over the little airstrip.

After flying into the interior, Burleigh saw the airstrip and also the missionaries down below. They were waving—waving him off—not to land. Things were too tense for him to come in. The missionaries on the ground saw Burleigh turn his aircraft away, then they saw a strange thing. He hesitated. Then he turned back and came straight into the little airport. He could not leave them there to die.

After he landed, one of the Congolese soldiers grabbed the keys to the plane, and in his excitement, Burleigh violated one of the laws of the jungle. He touched the soldier in trying to get the keys back, and the soldier shot him. Just before he died, Burleigh told the other missionaries, "Don't hold it against him. I shouldn't have touched him."

Back in the seventeenth century, there was a man who was writing about prayer. You would think that 400 years ago he had modern airplanes in mind. He wrote, "When Christ comes upon a soul, he needs a quiet landing place." I think Burleigh Law had it. Even in the midst of turmoil, he had inside himself a quiet landing place.

So, maybe we do not know how to pray, but that should not stop us. The disciples did not know how to pray. Paul did not know how to pray, either, but he did pray constantly. When he did, he found that God's spirit would intercede, perhaps with a sigh, and help him pray.

###

CHAPTER 7

Faith CAN Overcome Weariness

THE POWER TO USE YOUR TIREDNESS

Certainly faith can overcome weariness! For a great host of people, tiredness is a religious problem. That is not the whole story, of course. For some, tiredness is an organic problem, and those people should see a physician. Others are weary because, simply, they do not get enough rest. Still others have a chemical imbalance, which medication often helps. But for many, tiredness is a religious problem.

In the middle of the winter, most of us are convinced that what we really need is some kind of a break. We relieve the situation by going to Hawaii or Arizona or Florida or by having an affair or by yelling at the kids more than usual. On the other hand, summer is a time when our pace slows down. We play golf, and we wind down our committee work. We have cookouts and vacations, and sometimes we stop going to church, because it seems too much like the uptight winter schedule. Even though we have cookouts, golf, and vacations, often we still have a weariness that is not physical.

When Jesus was here on earth, he evidently encountered a lot of people like that. He said, "Come to me, all who labor and are heavy laden, and I will give you rest. Take my yoke upon you and learn from me . . . and you will find rest . . . . For my yoke is easy and my burden is light (Matthew 11:28–30)."

Burden? Yoke? In Palestine, an ox yoke fits one particular ox. Perhaps Jesus was speaking from his own experience working in his father's carpenter shop, where he learned the importance of making his ox yokes fit so they did not chafe or rub. They were positioned properly and fit well. Perhaps he is saying to us that whatever God sends us is made to fit our needs and abilities and that the task God has for each of us is made to measure for us.

The Menninger Clinic in Topeka, Kansas, occasionally has workshops for professionals in mental health sciences. Usually there is an interesting mix of physicians, both general practitioners and psychiatrists, social workers, psychologists, and ministers. We listen to addresses by Menninger staff, then have discussions in small groups on whatever the subject happens to be.

We heard a talk in which one of the staff psychiatrists said, "Most of the patients in my practice need something beyond themselves to tie to, something beyond themselves to serve." We were now in our small group talking. One of the physicians, a general practitioner, was asked, "What's the most frequent complaint your patients have?"

He answered, "The most frequent complaint by far is this, 'Why am I so tired?' You'd be surprised at the ones who ask that question. It isn't just the elderly or the infirm. Often as not it's younger men and women, people in their prime who really don't have anything physically wrong with them." A couple other doctors also said that one of their most frequent questions is about being tired. We all thought that was a little strange, since we have so many labor saving devices: automatic washing machines, dryers, dishwashers, vacuum cleaners, automobiles, even garage door openers. Shouldn't we have MORE energy to spend on other things?

Everyone in the group knew that there are many causes for tiredness: organic problems, of course, or chemical imbalance, or sometimes it is sanitation or diet or exercise or just not enough rest. Then one of the group brought up something the speaker of the morning had said, "There is nothing more delicate than the interrelation and interaction of body and soul. There are a considerable number of patients," he said, "who have nothing wrong with them except a certain 'world weariness.'" Then the speaker used a Greek word, Akedia, not caring. There are people, he said, "who just . . . don't . . . give . . . a . . . damn."

The story is told that Thomas Edison, the great inventor, worked 16 hours a day year in and year out. One July evening when he came home from work, his wife said, "You've worked long enough without a rest. You must go on a vacation."

"But where will I go?"

"Why don't you decide the place you'd rather be than anywhere else on earth. Go there for a vacation."

"Very well," Edison said, "I'll go there tomorrow. " The next morning Edison returned to his laboratory.

Maybe what we need is some devotion, something to lift us out of ourselves. We have all known times when we are too tired to clean out the basement, but we go to the golf course and energetically play 18 holes. You *know* that is true! Or you ask your children to mow the lawn, and they complain of great fatigue, "Had a hard day," etc. Five minutes later, an invitation comes to shoot baskets or go to a pool party or to a dance, and your son or daughter, too tired to mow the lawn, will shoot baskets or swim or dance for hours with no sign of fatigue.

Or you yourself come home tired after a long day at the office. You are so tired you can scarcely get out of the car and tumble onto the sofa. Then your child has a bad fall, and you have to rush him to emergency at the hospital, and for some reason you have unlimited energy. Our bodies are never too tired to do what our minds are interested in doing.

At the age of 45, a man went to consult a psychologist because he was always tired. In his early years, he had worked constantly without fatigue as a dishwasher, a delivery boy, a furnace tender, and in the summer as a laborer on a construction crew. He did all these things to get an education. At last he got a fine job as a chemist and settled down to a quiet, comfortable, uneventful life. He joined a church, then dropped out. Once he had played the violin with considerable pleasure and skill, but in the last five years, he had not touched it. He and his wife did not have children, and increasingly they lived a selfish, ingrown life. In the early years, when he was struggling against odds, he felt great. Now, with every comfort and security, he was "all in" at the slightest exertion.

The psychologist the man consulted happened to be a Christian, and he saw that the man had had energies to burn at one time, but now his excess energies were burning him up instead. Here was a man who did not have children, friends, or committees to worry about, so he was forced to worry about himself.

Clinical tests have proved that much of our modern exhaustion is due more to an excess of energy than to a lack of it.

William James, America's great pioneer psychologist, says, "Never allow yourself to have an emotion without expressing it afterward in some active way. Let the expression be the least thing in the world, speaking cheerfully to your grandmother, or doing someone a favor at the office, if nothing more heroic presents itself. But never fail to let it take place."

Harry Overstreet, who is a psychologist and also a Christian, says, "Say a decent word to your mother-in-law. Give an extra quarter to the waiter. Take your wife out to dinner. Otherwise the emotions, feeding only on themselves, turn into toxins."

It is interesting that when Jesus was physically exhausted, instead of sleeping late the next morning, he often went to a quiet place to pray. Luke says that "great multitudes came together to hear Jesus, and after healing them of their infirmities he withdrew into the wilderness and prayed." On another occasion, Jesus was on a preaching mission and returned, evidently tired and discouraged because his message had not been received. He had just prayed with his disciples, and almost as an afterthought he said, "Come to me all who labor and are heavy laden, and I will give you rest. Take my yoke," that massive piece of wood placed over an oxen's neck so he can pull a heavy load. "Take my yoke on you and you will find rest for your souls, for my yoke . . . fits . . . well (Matthew 11:28–30)."

Awhile ago, there was a squib in *Sports Illustrated* about a poll taken of 1,000 football fans. "When you watch football on TV," they asked, do you usually drink beer or not?" Twenty-seven percent of the respondents said yes, 70% said not, and 3% said they did not know. That 3% is interesting, is it not? Do we get so confused or bored or irritable that we do not know whether or not we are drinking beer when we are watching football on TV? Maybe it would help if we had something or someone beyond ourselves to put a purpose to it all. In other words, we religionists would say that we need a God to serve. We need to get ourselves out of the spotlight.

Okay, let's say that is true. We agree to all of that. Still, the difficult question is, "How do we do it?"

Some years ago, the Mayo Clinic found what they termed "a new cure" for getting over that tired feeling. Their tests had revealed that many people are chronically tired—not because of an expenditure of energy but because they are living an unbalanced life. They took Dr. Richard Cabot's well-known formula and made a cross of four arms of equal length to represent the ideal life: work, play, love, and worship.

They said, " . . . when one or more of these arms are only stubs, the result is unhappiness, which is a frequent forerunner of fatigue." Thus, a businessperson's cross may have overlong work and love arms. A young person may be long on play and short on work. An elderly person who is alone may be long on work and worship but short on love and play.

For happiness, the Mayo Clinic said that the four arms must be equal: work, play, love, and worship. Dr. James Hatfield confirms this when he says, "Speaking as a student of psychotherapy I am convinced that the Christian religion is one of the most valuable and potent influences that we possess for producing that harmony . . . which is needed to bring health and power."

During a flu epidemic, all the staff and medical personnel of a hospital were working extremely long hours. One head nurse found herself obliged to work 20 out of 24 hours, and at the end of the week, she was so worn out that one Saturday night she said to herself, "I must consult a nerve specialist or . . ." She did not know why she suggested an alternative. She had not been to a religious service in years, but she added, "I must consult a nerve specialist . . . or go to church." The next morning one of her nurses saw her leaving the hospital and protested that she should be in bed. Instead, she walked a few blocks to a nearby church and had her thoughts redirected to spiritual channels. She was renewed and returned to work physically energized.

Remember that when Jesus became exhausted from the pressure of the crowds or was facing a difficult ordeal, he did not go to bed. He withdrew to a hillside and spent the night in prayer.

One of the sights of Boston today is Trinity Church on Copley Square. For many years, its minister was Phillips Brooks, who became a bishop of the Episcopal Church. He was an able writer, an excellent preacher, and the composer of our Christmas carol, "O Little Town of Bethlehem."

In his twenties, Brooks was a young giant, six-foot-three, which was quite tall several generations ago. When Brooks became a minister, ordinary effort exhausted him. Even small changes in the weather tired him. Then came a miracle. Within a year or two, his muscular strength quadrupled, and nothing could fatigue him. Year in and year out he preached three times on Sunday and several times during the week, easily carrying the heavy burden of parish work.

Whenever I go to Boston, I try to stop at Trinity Church and see the statue of Brooks just beyond the south side of the church. The sculptor had, I think, put the secret of Brooks' miraculous change into bronze. If you look carefully, you see standing behind Brooks is the figure of Jesus.

Phillips Brooks was, he thought, about to lose his mind worrying about himself. The moment he lost himself in service to someone greater and better than himself, he became possessed with a peace, confidence, and power that he had never known before.

When your mind is mastered by something greater than itself, it is relieved of *the intolerable, unbearable burden of yourself.*

So let us be Christian awhile longer and go along with the believers: the unsophisticated, the people who, in spite of everything, believe there is a purpose and that we are not alone on the road of life. Remember the words of that psychiatrist at the workshop mentioned earlier, "We need something beyond ourselves to serve. We need something beyond ourselves to tie to."

###

CHAPTER 8

The Survival of the Fierce

THE POWER TO PREVAIL

It's a jungle out there, we say, so we claw our way to survive: grasping, hurting, and slashing out at all who stand in the way. Contrast that with the words of Jesus, "If anyone wishes to come after me, let him deny himself and take up his cross . . . " Deny himself? Take up his cross and follow me?

St. Matthew probably wrote those words sometime between 80 and 90 A.D., which was the time of the bitterest persecution of Christians. He seemed to be saying that the time may come when it is possible to save your life by abandoning your faith. If you do, though, you are really losing life.

It is still true today that the person who meets life constantly expecting to be safe, secure, comfortable, and trouble free actually is losing all that makes life worthwhile. It was the psychiatrist Rollo May, who wrote in his book, *Modern Man In Search Of Himself*, "Never has a generation been so preoccupied with themselves, troubled about themselves, trying to find themselves." God gave us a life to spend, not to keep, and we never really can be happy when we are using life mostly for ourselves.

Of course, we are born self-centered. As babies, everything exists for us, but when we carry this self-centeredness into adult life, it becomes unhealthy. We ask, though, "Self preservation, isn't that nature's first law? Isn't it true that the first law of nature is to save ourselves?" Even if that were true, the real question is, HOW are we to save ourselves? By fighting fiercely in the rat race?

Remember, though, that in the story of evolution, it was not the fiercest fighters who survived. All those gigantic fighters are not around anymore. The Saber-Tooth Tiger, Triceratops, Wooly Mammoth, and Tyrannosaurus Rex—they are all gone.

But we are here! That tiny speck named humanity survived. Why? Because we have a brain and learned to cooperate with the elements and the animals and the planet. We began to trade, to merchandise, and to market on an international scale, which is another way of sharing instead of fighting.

During World War II, the young wife of a medical doctor served with her husband in India. When he died, she lost all interest in life. On the ship back to America, there was a seven-year-old boy whose parents had been killed in Burma. He tried to be a friend, but she avoided him. Then one night the ship was torpedoed, and she wanted to go down with the ship. Nearby she saw the boy shivering. He came to her, and for days in the south Pacific, they pulled each other through.

One of our best known clinical psychologists had ignored religion for many years. Then he discovered exactly what Jesus meant when he talked about finding life by giving it. He said he learned from his own practice that the self sparing life is the self defeating life. When people try to protect themselves by withdrawing from the risks and hurts and demands of life, invariably they diminish the self they are trying to protect.

The first law of life is not self-preservation. The first law of life is love. In fact, we need to love, even more than we need to BE loved. To preserve life, we must spend it on something.

The words of Jesus continue to confront us, "If anyone wishes to come after me, let him deny himself and take up his cross and follow me . . ." But there is more! Jesus also said, "Whoever wishes to have a safe life will lose it, and whoever loses his life for my sake will . . ."

Will what? We are going to discuss that in the next chapter entitled, "Get Lost!"

###

CHAPTER 9

Get Lost!

THE POWER TO WIN BY LOSING

A problem all of us have today is the conflict between self-loving and self-losing. Jesus said that we are to love our neighbors as ourselves, and overly-pious persons have been telling us that we are to love others MORE than we love ourselves. In Sunday school, I was taught to say, "God first, others next, and self last."

Jesus never said that! He said you should love your neighbor—not more, not less, but—AS you love yourself. The evil, you see, is not self love. We MUST love ourselves, respect ourselves, before we can love others. The problem, then, is not self love but self centeredness and self worship—and that is a lot different.

There was a monk named Telemachus who lived in the late fourth century. He thought the way to find life was to pray, meditate, and fast. He went into the desert and lived alone, trying to find nothing but contact with God. However, he felt something was wrong. One day he rose from his knees and began to think that the life he was living was not selfless but very selfish. The only thing in his life was to find God just for himself. He then decided that if he was to serve God, he also must serve people. The desert was no place for a Christian, because the cities were where the people lived.

Telemachus left the desert and went to Rome. Now, by this time, Rome was officially Christian, but they did many things that were not Christian. One was the gladiatorial games. Christians were no longer thrown to the lions, but prisoners captured in war had to kill each other to entertain the people.

How the Romans loved the games! They roared with blood lust as the gladiators fought. One day, Telemachus went to the games and arrived just as the chariot races were ending. There were 80,000 people waiting almost breathlessly for the gladiators. They marched in, presented themselves to the Emperor, and said, "Hail Caesar, we who are about to die salute you."

The fight was on. Telemachus was appalled by what he saw. People for whom Christ had died were killing themselves to amuse citizens who were supposed to be Christian! Suddenly, Telemachus jumped over the barriers and ran between the gladiators, trying to stop them. For a moment, the fight did stop, but the crowd started shouting, "Go, go, go!" The gladiators pushed the old man aside, but again he jumped between them, and the crowd began to throw stones at him. They yelled to kill him and get him out of the way, and a gladiator's sword flashed. Telemachus, in his hermit's robe, lay dead.

In an instant, the crowd went silent. They were shocked that a holy man should have been killed that way. Then they realized what this killing really was. The games ended abruptly that day and never began again. Gibbon, the historian, said the death of Telemachus did more for humankind than his life on the desert ever had.

I suppose we are not likely to be called on either to live a life of solitary prayer out in the desert or to jump between gladiators in the Colosseum in Rome.

The New Testament speaks of the death of self, the denial of self, and the losing of self to find life. This process sometimes is called salvation. In reality, it is deliverance from self-centeredness. The pioneer Swiss psychiatrist, Carl Jung, says the ONLY way to mental health is by self-giving. We save ourselves by losing ourselves.

If you want to make a speech, get lost. Lose yourself in the speech. Do not think of you; think of the speech. If you want to win friends and influence people, get lost. Get yourself off your mind. A person never does so poorly for himself as when he thinks about himself too much.

Everyone knows the best way to make the varsity in sports is to spend energy, train, and sacrifice. We know all that, but when it comes to religion, we become sentimental, even unrealistic. We go around putting a soft hand on people's shoulders, muttering pious little phrases. "Don't worry, everything's going to be all right," we say, when it is NOT going to be all right, unless some solutions are found, and some changes are made.

Go through the teachings of Jesus, and you will find some beautiful, lovely things there. There also is a realistic facing of universal spiritual laws. You simply cannot sentimentalize Jesus, "who could stir people to loyalty so intense they willingly would die for him," as Harry Emerson Fosdick wrote, "and others to hatred so fierce they would not rest until they had killed him."

Jesus was right—life lived to the fullest is lived by spending. For instance, we cannot say to our memory, "Look, memory, I'll need you when I'm old, so I will not use my mental muscles now." Fact is, if we do not use our memory now, we will not have it later. Our mind will be flabby. We live by the law of expenditure.

The Christian faith is not so much an ethic or a philosophy as a commitment. It does not mean that if we pledge allegiance to Jesus we will find business success or advantage in our studies or popularity or even a smooth life. It does mean we will have the peace and power of God, firmness, stability, and equilibrium. The Christian faith means doing what we can, not what we cannot.

Katharine Brush has written a story called *A Lodging for the Night*. A man named John Wintringer was involved in an automobile accident on a highway in Illinois and was taken to a hospital. An account of the accident appeared in the local paper, and the next day a Mrs. Malcolm Corwin, whose name he did not recognize, came to see him with her small son, Billy. "You don't remember me, do you?" she asked. "I'll never forget how kind you were to Malcolm and me in the hotel that night in New York during World War II." Then Wintringer recalled the overcrowded hotel, the young lieutenant in the waiting line for the registration desk, and the girl in the nearby chair.

Wintringer had a reservation and checked into the hotel in the afternoon, but the young lieutenant kept losing his place in line to some superior officer who outranked him. When the lieutenant arrived at the desk, there were no rooms left. Wintringer wanted to do something for the young couple, so he went to the manager's office and pleaded their case. There really were no rooms left, so he asked the manager to divide his room with a screen and set up an extra cot. He gave the couple a duplicate key and said he was going out to dinner and would not be back until after midnight. He would slip in quietly and sleep on the cot. When he awoke in the morning, the young lieutenant and his wife were gone, and there was a note on the pillow thanking him for being so kind.

Now, seven years later, in the hospital room in this Midwestern town, here was the girl again with a sheaf of homegrown flowers that the little boy was holding. The boy had brown eyes, a snub nose, and curly hair. Wintringer told him, "You look just like your father." Then he turned to the girl and said, "How is your husband?"

The girl said, "He didn't get back. He was killed in the Hurtgen Forest. That's the reason I'll never forget what you did for us. He was shipping out the next morning. That was the last time I ever saw him."

We sometimes think we could do a great deal more if we were stronger, if we were married, or if we were unmarried. Yet, God always asks us to do the things we CAN do. We can give significant (for us) sums of money for God's work. More importantly, perhaps, we could approach some of our heathen neighbors and persuade them to go to church with us. We can refuse to complain. We can stop pitying ourselves. We can be cheerful.

We say peace is important, but what can we do to stop fighting between nations? Even so, there are wars between husband and wife, between relatives, between races and classes, and between business competitors. Perhaps we could do something here. We could find ourselves by losing ourselves.

We could refuse to do unethical deeds, even though it might mean losing our job or a promotion. We could give up a little of our luxury because we want to use more of our money to help other people. These things are not easy, but we COULD do them. We could get ourselves out of the center and put God there.

So God does not ask us to do the good we cannot do. He asks us to do the good we can do. Do not hoard your heart. Give it away!

Get lost!

"He who would save his life shall lose it, and he who loses his life for my sake will keep it to life eternal."

###

CHAPTER 10

Chasing Success—
Whatever That Is

THE POWER TO BE SIGNIFICANT

All of us want to be successful. Of course we do! And yet, so few understand HOW or even WHAT is success. Alfred Adler, one of the major figures of early psychiatry, said what humans need most of all is to feel significant. Jesus agreed. He wanted us to be great. He admired energy, enthusiasm, and competence and thought this drive within us was one of the most valuable possessions, if we used it correctly.

> A school teacher named Janet Thompson had a student named Teddy Stallard, whom she just did not like. He seemed to have little interest in school. His clothes were messy, and his hair was uncombed. His records indicated a poor home situation: mother seriously ill, father without interest. Then there was a phrase that got to Janet Thompson, "Could do better." Christmas came, and the boys and girls in Miss Thompson's class brought her presents. They piled them on her desk and crowded around to watch her open them.

Among the presents was one from Teddy Stallard, which surprised her. Teddy's present was wrapped in brown paper and was held together with scotch tape. Inside was a gaudy rhinestone bracelet with half the stones missing and a bottle of cheap perfume. The other boys and girls began to giggle and smirk, but she silenced them by trying on the bracelet and putting some of the perfume on her wrist. "Doesn't it smell lovely?" she asked. At the end of the day, when the other children had left, Teddy lingered behind. He came over to her desk and said softly, "Miss Thompson . . . Miss Thompson, you smell just like my mother . . . and her bracelet looks real pretty on you." After he left, a tear formed in the corner of her eye, and she asked God to help her do better with Teddy.

By the end of the school year, Teddy showed dramatic improvement. He had caught up with most of the students and was ahead of some. She did not hear from him for a long time. Then one day she received a note that read: "Dear Miss Thompson, I wanted you to be the first to know. I will be graduating second in my class. Love, Teddy Stallard."

Four years later, another note arrived: "Dear Miss Thompson, they just told me I will be graduating first in my class. I wanted you to be the first to know. The university has not been easy, but I liked it. Love, Teddy Stallard." And four years later: "Dear Miss Thompson, as of today I am Theodore Stallard, M.D. How about that? I wanted you to be the first to know. I am getting married next month. Would you come and sit where my mother would sit if she were alive. You are the only family I have now. Dad died last year. Love, Teddy Stallard."

Well, what is success? In America we would say the president of a corporation is a success or the great running backs in football or rock stars, perhaps. Even in school, a successful student is the president of this or that, the one who is elected to a certain fraternity or sorority, or the one who makes a varsity athletic team.

Now, do not misunderstand me. I am not knocking the desire to be significant. I am just stating it. In fact, not long ago I was amused in visiting the new national headquarters of one of our larger denominations. The head of the denomination had the only office with four windows, and division leaders had three windows each and, very mathematically, every national church official had the number of windows that designated his or her relative importance. We understand that. That is the way corporate buildings are built and religious ones as well.

I have a friend who says that if all the automobiles in the United States were lined up bumper to bumper across the nation, 93% of the drivers immediately would pull out to pass. We all want to BE somebody, but the trouble is, we cannot agree on what BEING SOMEBODY actually means.

Our homes are status symbols, as are cars, boats, and travel. Even power lawn mowers, the riding kind, are part of the package. Something like that happened a few years ago in the Linde household. We had a fine black and white TV set that worked very well, but the Linde boys were ashamed that we did not have a color TV. We explained many times that we had many more important uses for our money.

"But, dad, EVERYBODY has color TV nowadays!"
"Well, we like this one just fine."
"Oh, dad!"

Do you remember times like that? We did not give in, either, until we discovered that the Linde boys were depositing themselves around the neighborhood, watching television on their friends' color sets, while our humble black and white set was boycotted.

So what is success? Certainly our goals change at different ages or in different conditions. A mother might say, "Success means having my teenager turn out well." Another mother would say, "Now that my role as a mother is finished, success is finding the best direction for the rest of my life."

There is a story in the Book of Matthew that tells about two disciples who wanted to be successful. It tells us, "And Jesus and his disciples were on the road going up to Jerusalem . . . and James and John, the sons of Zebedee, came to him and said,

"Teacher, we want you to do something for us."
"What is it you want me to do?"
"Oh, well . . . uh . . . oh, you tell him, John."
"Yes, well, it's like this. When you come into your kingdom, let one of us sit on your right hand, and the other on your left. When you are the king, I'd certainly like to be vice monarch, and James, here, wants to be secretary of foreign affairs. We've talked about it and . . . "

Jesus explained that whoever would be great must be a servant, and whoever would be first must be a slave, but they could not quite understand. When the other disciples heard about the incident, they were sour and sulked all the way to Jerusalem. Even when they entered the Upper Room for their last meal with Jesus, they still had long faces.

According to custom, when they entered a room such as this, they were supposed to have a servant wash off their dusty feet. Since there was not any servant, everyone tried to cover up his dirty feet with his robe and sniffed, "Not me, I'm not going to do a SERVANT'S work."

Then they heard the splash of water and looked around. There was Jesus pouring water into a bowl and taking a towel and putting it over his arm, like a servant. He began to wash the dust of the road off the disciples' feet, but Peter said, "Oh, no, no, Lord . . . uh, no, you can't do that for me . . ."

What is success? James and John had their own ideas—being successful was being important people in the new kingdom of God. Jesus had an entirely different thought: "Whoever would be great," he said, "must be a servant." An important question to be answered, though, is who rates our success? Society? Certainly. Prime ministers are important people, as are secretaries of states, those who occupy the corner offices of executive suites, and football stars. We prove that by paying them top dollar.

Parents can have a great influence on our own success ratings. Bob Raines is a minister and writer who said that in his family there were three boys. His father was a bishop in the Methodist Church, and all three boys went to seminary to study for the ministry. He said, "It could be there was a substantial blast from the Holy Spirit operating in our family, but it could also be that there was a very powerful, if loving pressure in our family."

Raines then said that his father was his role model for many years, both personally and professionally, but only in recent years has he consciously begun to own himself and choose his vocation.

There is, in fact, some evidence that our ideas of success in America are changing. A report entitled *The Changing Success Ethic*, published by the American Management Association, gives a survey of several thousand business people. It indicates that the idea of success is moving away from the accumulation of material goods to other, less tangible objectives, such as "quality of life."

A businessman was telling his associates about attending a lunch with several prominent citizens. Suddenly, one man looked them in the eye and said, "Do you consider yourselves to be successful?" One-by-one, each replied positively, perhaps too quickly, but several were thinking that a more honest response might have been "Yes, but . . . ," or "I'm not sure anymore what success means for me."

It is true that our ideas of success change at different ages or at different levels of our careers. The same situation is often graded differently by different people.

A man was on a business trip to Jamaica, and outside his hotel there were two good looking black boys playing with a rope. The businessman came out of the hotel and thought he would have some fun. He drew a line between the boys and told them they would get a dollar every time they pulled the knot in the rope across the line. There would be a tug of war, he thought, with gruntings and groanings, but that is not what happened. There was some music somewhere with a Caribbean beat, and with an easy dance step, the boys took the knot back and forth across the line many times. In just a few minutes they had made ten dollars each for themselves.

Ultimately, though, we give ourselves our grades on success. At a recent workshop, a young man had his own successful business but said he left it to work with native Americans at a considerably lower income. He said, "Success in my life is contingent on my enabling others to identify success in their lives." A social service worker who enjoyed working with people who have problems was offered a promotion as an administrator but turned it down because she knew that, for her, it would not be any fun. As someone once said, "Success is inside us more than what we achieve out there." Or this, "We become somebody, not in what belongs to us, but in the ideals we belong to."

A book entitled *Unworld People* by Joyce Lansdorf tells about a local edition of The Special Olympics for the handicapped. When the 220 yard race was called, these special children lined up. Then the gun sounded. It was a good start, and the runners were off just as they are in the real Olympics, legs pumping and arms churning down the track. Then one of the children toward the back of the pack tripped, stumbled, and fell, skidding through the cinders. It was a painful scene. The crowd gasped, and the other runners went on for maybe ten yards before one of them noticed what had happened. Awkwardly, he stopped and went back to help the unfortunate boy. Soon another did the same, then another, and another, until all the racers were clustered around their friend, dusting the dirt from his shirt, patting him on the back, and affirming him.

Strangely, nobody ever finished the race! But then, maybe they did. Maybe they all did . . . maybe they all won.

###

CHAPTER 11

But I've Gotta Eat!

How Much Security Does a Person Need?

An article in *The Wall Street Journal* noted that most chief executives believe success in their careers demands they make personal sacrifice, and most put their jobs ahead of their families and themselves. This article was reporting a survey done jointly by *The Wall Street Journal* and the Gallup organization and said, "The heads of the 1,300 largest U.S. companies work 60 to 70 hours a week, and give up many of their weekends . . . They accept as necessary their rigorous work schedules."

Many agree with that, but we phrase it a little differently. We say, "But I've gotta eat!" We know that is a patent falsehood, though. We have far more than our families can consume. In fact, most of us are on diets. Others say, "If I don't look out for myself, who will?" While that may be true, the real problem is that we do not want to be left behind, whether it is in providing for our families or taking nice vacations or sending our kids to college or being in love or getting a promotion.

Long ago, Lev Tolstoy, the Russian writer, told about a peasant farmer named Pahom, who was always wanting more land. He would save a few rubles and buy land, again and again. Then he heard that in the far off land of the Bashkirs there was plenty of land, and they would sell it cheaply. He made the long trip and talked with the chief of the Bashkirs.

"Yes, it is true," the chief said. "We will sell as much land as you can walk around in a day, and the price is 1,000 rubles. But if you do not return to the starting point before the sun sets, you lose both your money and the land."

Pahom was delighted. At sunrise he started out. He walked through flat land black for farming, a damp hollow for flax, a stream he wanted to include, and a woodland. Before Pahom realized it, the sun was nearing the horizon, and he had to summon all his strength to return to the starting point before sunset.

Puffing, gasping for breath, with his last ounce of strength he ran, at last plunging into the midst of the Bashkirs waiting at the starting point. They all applauded, and the chief made a speech. When Pahom did not move, they turned him over. He was dead. The Bashkirs dug a grave just long enough for Pahom and buried him there.

"But then," Tolstoy concluded, "how much land does a man need?"

One of the founders of Burrswood Hospital in England was Marina Chavchavadze, a former Russian princess. Marina's family fled the revolution in Russia and arrived penniless in England. Her greatest fear was that never again would she have the means to live graciously and comfortably. Very early in her life, as a refugee, she vowed, "I'll never marry a poor man. I refuse to darn socks and clean rooms and do domestic chores.

But," she asked, "what do you think the Lord did? He brought me here to Burrswood to clean floors and scrub and cook. He knew my fear was hindering me, and I ended up enjoying it. Once I began to enjoy it, I was released from my fear."

But I've gotta eat? Well, maybe. After years of counseling and dealing with people, I am convinced that most people are miserable because they choose to be miserable.

Oh?

Most of us do not think that. We are sure that if we could just be in love with the right person, be married, be unmarried, lose weight, or change the color of our skin, everything would be okay.

Certainly those things are important, and yet one of the basic truths about us human beings is that our happiness and completeness come from within.

Abraham Maslow, one of our motivational psychologists, says that all humans have the same kinds of needs. At the base of his pyramid of needs are the physiological: food, water, clothing, and shelter. Just above that are the safety needs: security, stability, freedom from fear, and freedom from anxiety. When we satisfy those needs, according to Maslow, we need love and belonging: relationships, affections, neighborhood, and community. Then he says we want esteem, self-respect, and the admiration of others. At the very top of our needs, though, is self-actualization. In other words, we need to do that for which we are best suited.

The Romans had a proverb that said money is like sea water. The more a person drinks, the thirstier he becomes.

In the Gospel according to Luke, Jesus says, "Watch and guard against the spirit which is always wanting more, for even if a person has an abundance, his life does not come from his possessions." Then he tells about a rich farmer who had a bumper crop one year, and even though he had extensive storage facilities, he did not know what to do with his wealth. He decided to tear down his barns and build bigger ones.

What is wrong with it?

For one thing, the Lord in the parable called the man a fool. Jesus went on to say, "Don't worry so much about your life. Can you by worrying add a few inches to your height?" What Jesus is trying to tell us is there is another world out there, and we do not think much about it.

There is a story about a conversation an ambitious young man had with an older man. The young man began by saying,

"I'll learn my trade."
"And then?"
"I'll set up in business."
"And then?"
"I'll make my fortune."
"And then?"
"I suppose I'll grow old, retire, and live on my income."
"And then?"
"Well, I suppose some day I'll die."
"And then?"

So there is another world out there, a world of flowers and birds and sunsets. A world of God and the spiritual life. A world of other people, poor people, brown people, purple people, and dirty people. People we do not like very well.

Even if we do have a private jet, a classic Jaguar XKE, and a 48 inch rear projection HD television, there is a need that all these things do not satisfy. We have to live FOR something.

I am convinced that God is the force that integrates these needs of ours. Remember that Christianity began in a carpenter shop, surrounded by the common tools of daily life. When Jesus talked about religion, how different his jargon was from the stuffy language of the priests. He talked about flowers that were prettier than Solomon in his finery, and about children at play. He talked about vineyards and shepherds, about parties and weddings, about business and money, about the different kinds of soil, about the unemployed standing in the marketplace waiting to be hired, about friendship, and the changing colors in the evening sky. It did not sound like temple religion at all.

No wonder the priests hated him.

So when we stop reading these words and lay the book down and go out among people, we bump head first into a world that does not believe in all that stuff Jesus was talking about. Can truth be sacred, when we are often expected to lie for personal advancement? Can beauty be sacred, when sex is constantly exploited? Can office parties be sacred? Can the rat race be sacred?

Yes, these things CAN be sacred. They may not be sacred now, but they can be. Listen:

> In the 19th century, it was said that Edwin Booth ran a theatre with integrity and character. Back in those days, there were a lot of church members who thought it was wrong to attend the theatre. One cowardly minister wanted to attend Booth's theatre without being seen himself. So he wrote Edwin Booth and asked if there was a back or side door in the theatre where he could slip in without being observed. Booth wrote back, "There is no door in my theatre through which God cannot see."

No door in my theatre, my business, my recreation, or my home through which God cannot see. That is real religion.

So preparing a balance sheet can be sacred, if business is a stewardship. Aerobic exercises can be sacred, for our bodies are temples of God. Sweeping the floor can be sacred, for it is keeping God's creation orderly. Healing can be sacred. Sex can be sacred, for God gave it to us. Parties can be sacred, for they are a celebration of the life God gave us.

Here were some fishermen on the Sea of Galilee who, one day, saw and heard a remarkable person. Dirty, cussing fishermen, who started out at sunrise, pulled in as many fish as they could, then had to get the smelly catch to market before it spoiled in the hot Galilean sun. As Jesus spoke to them on the seashore, he did not sound like their scribes and religious leaders. Jesus awakened in them a divine discontent. He stirred in them the need to be something they never had dreamed of being. They said about it, "In him we have become new persons."

There was a little boy who was asked if he could play the violin. "I don't know," he replied, "I never tried it." We smile at that old story, because it is so ridiculous. But how will you know if Christianity actually works, unless you try it?

###

CHAPTER 12

Absolutely Essential, Impossible Neighbors

THE POWER TO LOVE THE UNLOVABLE

How do you love a person who has taken your job? How do you love a person who has intentionally put a long, deep scratch down the side of your beautiful, shiny new car? How can you love a nation, when you are at war with them? How can underprivileged people love a place where they are sure they are being discriminated against?

We love every one . . . but him, and him, and her.

Right after Jesus made his great statement that we must love God with our whole heart, soul, and mind, and our neighbor as ourselves, someone asked him, "Well, rabbi, just, ah, WHO IS MY NEIGHBOR?" Then Jesus let him have it. He said—and this is the way the story might be told if it took place today:

A man was going home from Denver to Colorado Springs, and some guys on motorcycles held him up. They had robbed him of his wallet and expensive watch, then beat him up, and drove off in his car, leaving him unconscious under an overpass on Interstate 25.

Now, it just so happened that a minister was passing that way, and he was hurrying to a meeting with the chaplain on pastoral care at Memorial Hospital. He was late, so when he saw the poor, unconscious fellow, he stepped on the gas and sped away.

The next person on the scene was a pre-law student at University of Colorado, Colorado Springs. He slowed down and looked at the man but remembered that he had to study for a final exam, so he shifted gears and drove off.

Then a young woman on welfare, driving a shiny, new Cadillac, on the way home from a Denver Broncos football game came upon the fellow, and what she saw caused her heart to fill with compassion. She stopped and bound up his wounds as best she could, got some water, and wiped away the blood. Then she put him in the backseat of her car and took him to the hospital. She said to the people at the admissions desk, 'Please take good care of this poor man, okay? And take this $100 bill—it is the only money I have right now—and anything his Blue Cross does not cover, I will settle up with you at the end of the month, when I get my welfare check."

Does that bother you: that woman on welfare in the shiny new Cadillac, handing over the $100 bill to the hospital?

Down in the southwest among the Mexican Americans, they tell the story a little differently, but it is the same story. In their folklore among the Mexican Americans, they have a character called Taco Tico. He is the no-good "sellout." He is an informer who sells information about Mexicans who cross the border into the United States illegally. He is despised. Taco Tico is the enemy.

The story continues:

A Mexican American is on the road to Santa Fe late at night. He has a flat tire and no spare. Soon a car comes along, with a priest hurrying to a midnight mass someplace. It does not stop. Another car drives by and does not stop. But a third one does stop, and inside, offering help, is Taco Tico, the enemy.

You see, Jesus' audience identified with this story, because for centuries, the Jews had thought of themselves as beaten, robbed, and left for dead. Then, as Jesus tells it, along come two members of the establishment, and of course, they do not stop to help. Then the enemy arrives, a collaborator, a sellout. A Samaritan.

We think too easily that we know just what Jesus' story of the Good Samaritan teaches: We should all go out and be Good Samaritans, right?

Wrong.

You see, Jesus was trying to get across a radical truth, not "What must I do?" That was not the question at all. The question Jesus was trying to answer was this, "Who is my neighbor?" He told a simple story about a man who was robbed and beaten and left in a ditch by the side of the road, and the only one who would help him is not a person he liked. It was a SAMARITAN!

A Samaritan. When the Jews were taken into captivity in Babylon, some Jews in Samaria stayed behind. They intermarried and raised up a bastard race. Samaritans were traitors. They went to the Jews' holy temple in Jerusalem with their animals and defecated there—IN THE TEMPLE! In the time of Jesus, no Jew would go through Samaria, because he might be killed!

Imagine the shock when Jesus said that it was a Samaritan who helped the beaten and robbed man lying in the ditch!

Today when someone asks the question, "Who is my neighbor?" often we do not want to hear the answer. Our neighbor could be someone we do not like: an old man who would not let me pass him on the Interstate or an accountant in our business who just does not interpret the balance sheet the way we do. Or it could be Fidel Castro or the KKK.

Awhile ago, I was in Houston lecturing at the Museum of Natural History, and I stayed at a hotel near the museum. When I walked into the lobby of this hotel, it was apparent I had walked in on a convention of Christian young people. The place was filled with them. They were eating there, sleeping there, and holding meetings in the public rooms.

As I looked around the lobby, it was crowded with good looking, clean, scrubbed young people—handsome young men, dressed elegantly with ties and sport jackets or even three piece suits. And what lovely young ladies! I have never seen such a collection of beautiful women. Both the young men and women had their hair cut just the right length and sprayed in exactly the right place. All so Christian, but with one exception.

I did not see one boy with acne or one girl who was overweight more than ten pounds. I did not see a black, brown, red, or yellow person. I sat down in one of the plush chairs in the lobby and began to think about it.

I could not help but wonder what would have happened if Jesus came through the hotel lobby doors in the company of those prostitutes and lepers he associated with, those stinking fishermen, and those infamous tax collectors with whom he spent so many hours.

I know that God is the God of the beautiful, talented people, but is he the God ONLY of beautiful, talented people? Is he not also the God of the people we dislike, the God of our enemy?

One minister I know had been going through a particularly rough time with a member of his congregation. The man had been trouble for no reason at all, it seemed. Every fence the minister tried to mend only encouraged the man to be more difficult. The minister was talking it over with a friend and exploded, "How in heaven's name am I supposed to love a man like that?"

The friend said, "You sound as though you expect yourself to be able to be fond of him, but that's nonsense. Fondness and affection for people is one thing, but Christian love is something different."

So many of us think love is church talk that never comes to grips with people as they are. But we do have impossible neighbors who are essential to us—the lout at the office who keeps needling me, the liar who conned me, the loud-mouth who barged into my neighborhood, or a friend who took advantage of my trust. By what magic am I supposed to feel anything but resentment or distrust and a justified desire to have nothing to do with them?

What if Christian love was never meant to mean the way we FEEL toward people? It's what we DO about these feelings that matters. The lout at the office, the liar, or the loud-mouth may not be our friends, but they are neighbors, because we cannot escape them.

In order to emphasize that idea, sometime at a communion service in your church you might use various kinds of bread instead of the usual type of wafer. There could be, all mixed together:

—taco chips from Spanish speaking Americans,
—corn bread from the poor people of the southern United States,
—bagels from our Jewish culture,
—dark bread our immigrant mothers and fathers might have baked,

—soda crackers representing elderly people who do not have enough income to eat well anymore

—hamburger buns from our young people, or

—rice crackers from the Orient.

Who is my neighbor?

One summer I heard Fred Craddock, the great teacher of preachers, tell a story about his own father, who did not go to church. He said, "My mother took us. Once in awhile, someone from the church would come and try to talk with my father. This made my mother nervous, for my father could talk pretty forcibly, if he was pushed. He'd say, 'The church doesn't care anything about me. You must want another pledge. What's the matter, budget a little low?'"

Dr. Craddock said he had heard these expressions a thousand times from his father, while his mother wept in the kitchen. But there was a time his father did not say it. He was in the Veterans' Hospital in Memphis, Tennessee. He had dropped to 71 pounds. "Cancer of the throat," they said. "You shouldn't have been smoking." They had taken out most everything surgically and put in a little metal tube. He could put his finger over it and make some noises, but mostly he would write.

"I walked into the room," Dr. Craddock said, "having flown in to see my father. In every window, flowers. By his bed, a stack of cards 20 inches deep. Even the table that swings out over the bed to put food on, fresh flowers. I looked at the cards beside his bed, and everyone of them from groups or persons in the church. He couldn't speak, so he got a Kleenex box and wrote on the side of it a line from Hamlet, 'In this harsh world draw your breath in pain and tell my story.'"

"I will, Dad, but what is it?"

And his father wrote, "I . . . WAS . . . WRONG!"

Then Craddock concludes, "Isn't it true. Haven't you found that wherever you go, wherever there's need, wherever you find distress, or pain, or bereavement, you'll find Christians who come bringing something, trying to be neighbors—a pie, a meatloaf, an offer of transportation, or care of children, something? People everywhere care."

###

CHAPTER 13

The New Hypocrisy

THE POWER TO BE GENUINE

L et us talk about pretending, since we all do it. Sometimes there is nothing wrong with it. There are times in life when everyone wears a mask. Psychologists, in fact, talk about "role playing," where we participate in actions that are expected of us.

A woman acts differently when she is entertaining guests for bridge than she does when she is home by herself in the evening after all the children are tucked safely in bed. Of course!

The boss acts differently when he's negotiating with employees than when he is with friends. Certainly!

Young people sometimes say that is "phony," but they, too, act one way with teachers and another way with students. Most people wear masks at times, and that is okay.

We have "virtual reality," which is not actually like the original but is so near to it that the difference is negligible. If we do not want to take the time to send a letter by ordinary mail, we can send a facsimile on a fax machine. A facsimile is not the original; it may be an exact copy, but it is still a copy.

We have "lite" ice cream that pretends to taste like the original without all the calories and fat content. It may be better for you, but it is not the "real stuff."

Now, we are talking about pretense, and pretense can be hypocrisy. Pretense also may NOT be hypocrisy. Webster says a hypocrite is a "person who pretends to be other or better than he or she is."

A woman who acts differently with her two o'clock bridge club than she does alone after a hard day may not be hypocritical. She may just be tired. The home that serves ice milk instead of ice cream may not be hypocritical. It may just be health conscious.

For instance, there was a medical student who was financing his education by working at two jobs over the summer. During the day, he worked in a meat market, and in the evening, he worked as an orderly in the operation room of a hospital. One night he was wheeling a lady patient into the surgery room, when she looked up at him and screamed, "Why . . . why . . . it's my butcher!" Now, the young man was not a hypocrite; he was a hard worker, carrying two jobs. The difference comes in pretense.

A hypocrite is a person who pretends to be other or better than he or she is. In the Greek origin of the word, "hupokrites" was an actor, one who played a part on the stage.

In the very beginning of his ministry, Jesus cautioned his disciples, "You must not be as the hypocrites are." Then he described hypocrites. They are Pharisees. They stand in the center of the marketplace when they say their prayers, so they can be seen. Jesus even tells a parable about two men going into the Temple to pray, "One was a Pharisee, and the other a tax collector."

"The Pharisee stood apart by himself and prayed, 'I thank you, God, that I am not greedy, dishonest, or an adulterer like everybody else. I thank you that I am not like that tax collector over there. I fast two days a week, and I give you one-tenth of my income.'"

Perhaps we should not be too hard on the Pharisees. In many ways, the Pharisees were the best people in the country. They spent their lives observing every detail of the law. And since there were regulations to govern every possible incident in every possible moment of life for every possible person—the Pharisees had their work cut out for them.

For instance, the Book of Jeremiah says, "Take heed to bear no burden on the Sabbath." So a burden had to be defined. It was "food equal in weight to a dried fig, milk enough for one swallow, honey enough to put on a wound . . . " The Pharisees dedicated their lives to keeping the law, and to a Jew of that time, THAT WAS BEING RELIGIOUS!

Now, "that tax collector over there"—he knew he was not righteous. Everyone told him so. A man purchased the right to collect taxes within a certain district. He was responsible to the Roman government for an agreed sum, but anything he could raise OVER that amount, he was allowed to keep. In those days, before newspapers and television, the people did not know how much they should pay in taxes, and they had no right of appeal against a tax collector. So, many tax collectors became wealthy through illegal extortion.

On the other hand, the Pharisee dedicated his life to keeping the law and was, therefore, a very . . . religious . . . person. He was, in fact, proud of his piety, because THAT WAS BEING RELIGIOUS! One rabbi, Simeon ben Jochai, once said, "If there are only two righteous men in the world, I and my son are these two. If there is only one, I am he!"

Back to Jesus' story: "The tax collector stood afar off and would not lift even his eyes to heaven and said, 'O God, be merciful to me the sinner.'" Not merely "a" sinner, but "the" sinner. And it was that heart-broken prayer that won the tax collector acceptance before God.

So Jesus ended his story, "I tell you, this man went down to his house accepted with God, rather than the other, because everyone who exalts himself will be humbled, but he who humbles himself will be exalted."

To illustrate, at the Yale School of Alcoholic Studies one summer, a medical doctor was giving a lecture on the bad physical effects of alcohol. He talked about what happens to blood pressure, nutrition, brain reaction, and so forth. One lady had been nodding her assent all through the lecture, and at one point she rose to her feet and asked, "After all you've said, doctor, is there any disease a total abstainer like myself could ever get, that an alcoholic doesn't?" The doctor thought a minute then said, "Only one, madam, and it is a bad one. It's called 'pressure of the halo.'"

For the Christian, this is one of the worst sins, to say, "I am not as other people are." These Christians have been described as "starched before they are thoroughly washed." Or as Mark Twain described such a person, he was "a good man in the worst sense of the word."

Up to this point, I suppose, many have been feeling pretty comfortable. No one likes a hypocrite, but the trouble is, ALMOST NO ONE SUSPECTS HE OR SHE IS A HYPOCRITE! "I may be many things, but at least I'm not a hypocrite. Not little old, humble me."

Harry Kruener, who used to be the chaplain at Denison University in Ohio, once said, "No one likes to be called a hypocrite. It's a mean word, and it's intended to hurt." Then he continues, "This happened to one student I know. He's a young man who gets up and goes to church on Sunday mornings. Most of the other fellows at the fraternity lie around and stay in bed Sunday mornings, and they call him a hypocrite because he goes. Of course," Kruener says, "the brothers at the fraternity should understand one thing: there really are two kinds of hypocrites. A hypocrite may be a person who pretends to be better than he really is, but a hypocrite may also be a person who pretends to be worse than he is . . . . The hypocrite may also be the one lying in bed . . . "

After all, what does the word "hypocrite" mean? One who plays a part, a pretender. The boy in bed also may be a pretender, pretending to be worse than he actually is. This is a great sin of our day, pretending—not to be better, but to be worse—than we actually are. This is "the new hypocrisy."

Some years ago, Bruce Marshall wrote a novel entitled *The World, The Flesh And Father Smith*. At one point in the story, Father Smith is talking with a Protestant minister:

> Father Smith says, "If we are really Christians there should be no occasion on which we are not gathered together in Christ's name. Christ should be in our ballrooms and theatres, just as he is in our churches. But we are afraid to be ourselves in crowds, and so everybody pretends to be less pious, less virtuous, less honorable that he or she really is."

The minister replies, "I think, with your permission, I shall use that in a sermon sometime."

> Then Father Smith continues, "It's what I call the new hypocrisy. In the old days people pretended to be better than they were, and now they pretend to be worse. In the old days a man said he went to church on Sunday, even if he didn't, but now he says he plays golf, and would be distressed if his men friends found out he really went to church." Father Smith concluded, "I think it is a very much worse state of affairs, because it means that . . . we no longer dare to be private, honest people; but instead are becoming the facades we pretend."

Jesus probably never saw this other type, the new style hypocrite. There is the business woman who sprinkles her conversation with a few cuss words, not because she likes the words but because she wants to be one of the gang. There is the man who tells people, "Well, I'm no angel," when, in fact, he is a pretty good guy. There is the teenager experimenting with drugs, partly out of curiosity but also because of peer pressure to be like everyone else.

A college professor paraphrased the parable of Jesus for our day by saying:

> Two students went to church on Easter to pray, the one a regular churchgoer, and the other a cool man of the world. And the man of the world prayed thus with himself, "God, I thank you that I am not as other people are, simple minded, narrow, inhibited, or even as this poor churchgoer. I get my religion two or three times a year, I give to the charity drives . . . I may look innocent, but, God, you know me, I get around."

You get the point: the sophisticated man of the world often is as much a hypocrite as the Pharisee. The Pharisee and the tax collector are still with us.

Studdert-Kennedy, the great British chaplain of World War I, told of a man who was a member of his civilian parish. The man was a fine man, but he was addicted to alcohol. Time after time, he tried to conquer his alcoholism but failed. For one period, he did not touch a drop for six months, then on Good Friday he got drunk.

The day afterward he was full of remorse. He came to Studdert-Kennedy and asked him if he could take communion on Easter. Kennedy asked him if he wanted to conquer his affliction, and the man, with moving sincerity, said he would give his right hand to be rid of it. Kennedy said that the Lord would be waiting for him, as he was for Peter after his denial.

A few days after Easter, a man stopped Studdert-Kennedy on the street and asked him about that sanctimonious so-and-so who got drunk on Good Friday then piously came to church and took communion on Easter. Then the man added, "He's no good. He's a hypocrite. When I want to take a drink, I do it and don't make any bones about it!"

Then Kennedy made a statement that, for me, has become the answer to our new breed of hypocrites. He said, "Anybody can profess to be a scoundrel and be one. But in the sight of God, there are just two kinds of people: those who are longing and striving to be better than they are, and those who are not."

Ultimately, Christ is the only true answer to this problem. I am convinced the Christian faith helps us to live beyond pretense. This is what Paul calls "the simplicity that is in Christ." Before God, we need wear no mask. We do not have to play a part. We do not have to pretend to be better or worse than we are.

And perhaps that is God's greatest gift to the Christian: the gift of being genuine.

###

CHAPTER 14

Do You WANT to Be Well?

THE POWER TO CHANGE

Illness is one of the inevitables of life. Sooner or later all of us are laid on the shelf, temporarily at least.

When our son, Rob, was a boy, he was scheduled for a tonsillectomy, and we prepared the way by explaining everything pleasantly and realistically. All seemed to be going well. We took him to the hospital, dressed him in a hospital gown, and joked a little with him. Then an orderly began pushing him in his bed down the hall toward the operating room. Suddenly Rob sat upright and said, "I think I'd like to go home now."

I suspect many of us are like that. We muster our courage as we face illness, but when the time comes for the ordeal, how we would like to go home!

The Gospel of John (5:1–18) tells about a man whom Jesus healed at the pool of Bethzatha. "After this there was a feast of the Jews, and Jesus went up to Jerusalem. In Jerusalem, near the sheepgate, there is a bathing pool with five porches, which is called in the Hebrew Bethzatha." This was a sunny spot on the edge of town where a person could get away from the city and just sit down in the sun or take a dip in the pool. Besides being a swimming pool and sun deck, Bethzatha was a spa for people with chronic ailments. The scripture continues, "In the porches there lay a crowd of people who were ill, and blind, and lame, and whose limbs were withered, waiting for the moving of the waters!"

Beneath the pool, there was a subterranean stream, and every now and then, the stream bubbled up and disturbed the waters of the pool. Some believed the disturbance was caused by an angel and that the first person to get into the pool after the angel troubled it would be healed of his illness.

As Jesus was walking around the Pool of Bethzatha, a man was pointed out who had been ill for 38 years. His disability made it unlikely, even impossible, to be the first to get into the pool after it had been disturbed. Jesus went up to the man. He did not try to lecture or counsel him, and according to the record, Jesus asked simply, "Do you want to be well?"

The man evaded Jesus' question and answered, "Sir, I have no one to take me quickly into the pool when the water is disturbed, so while I am on the way, someone gets there before me."

Jesus said, "Get up, fold your lounge chair and walk!" Yes, that is right—lounge chair. The Greek word is "krabbatos," which is a light stretcher-like frame similar to the ones we use on our patios today. The point is, the man was made well, and he folded his chair and walked.

Now enter the villains in the story. Jesus slipped away into the crowd, and Jews who were there began to accuse the man for CARRYING HIS CHAIR! According to Jewish law, he had no right to do that on the Sabbath. The rabbis of Jesus' day were so legalistic that they solemnly argued that a man was sinning, if he carried so much as a NEEDLE in his robe on the Sabbath. The actual words of the law were, "If anyone carries anything from a public place to a private house intentionally he is punishable by DEATH BY STONING!" So the healed man was in trouble. He had carried his lounge chair on the Sabbath.

The scripture ends with these words, "Because of this the Jews tried all the harder to find a way to kill Jesus, not only because he was habitually breaking the Sabbath, but also because he kept saying that God was his own father."

Today we are much better informed about medicine, but so often we expect it to perform miracles, while we sit back and do nothing. For instance, when tranquilizers were first announced, it seemed as though psychologists and counselors soon would be out of business. A person could take a pill and suddenly feel at peace with oneself and the world. However, many discovered these drugs gave only temporary relief but did nothing to resolve the conflict that caused the trouble in the first place.

Anyone who makes very many calls on sick people soon realizes the seriousness of a person's sickness has very little to do with cheerfulness. For instance, some people who are in incredible pain still are very pleasant, and others suffering from only trifling illness are the most grumpy. Could illness emphasize our true character?

There is a portrait of Robert Louis Stevenson, the writer, in which he is propped up in bed, covers drawn over his shrunken knees, playing the flute. He could play his flute and write immortal stories, pain or no pain.

Back to the "Jewish Community Center" of Jerusalem or what was then called the Pool of Bethzatha. Jesus asked the man if he wanted to be well, and immediately the man changed the subject. Instead of answering with a simple yes or no, the man began an irrelevant explanation about how it really was not his fault that he had been ill for 38 years. The reason was that he had no one to take him quickly to the pool when it bubbled, because God would heal only the first person in the water. "You see, Lord, it really isn't my fault!"

Let us look at that part of the story in the light of our modern care. Hospital personnel all know that two patients who have the same doctors and nurses in the same hospital with the same illness will react differently. One of the two says the meals are terrible, the nurses are inefficient, the hospital is disorganized, and the doctor does not know what he is doing. The other says the food is excellent, the nurses are wonderful, and the doctor is tops. That person is cheerful, full of hope, and quite often is making an excellent recovery, while the gloomy person is not doing so well.

So many of us like to say it is not our fault; it really is not! It is the fault of the nurses or the doctors or the dietician. Like the man at the Pool of Bethzatha, "I have no one to help me!"

Dr. Gerald Kennedy, who later became one of the country's great preachers and a bishop in the Methodist Church, says he remembers, when he was in high school, he went through a period of feeling sorry for himself. He knew boys and girls who had so many advantages he never had. They came from well-to-do families, but his parents were poor and lived in the wrong part of town. Surely, he thought, it would not be his fault if he could make nothing of his life.

Then Kennedy happened to reread the story of the Prodigal Son, who had gone into a far country and became poor, hungry, and defeated. He was slopping hogs, and for a Jew, that is about as low as you can get. Then the boy said he would go home to his father and say, "Father, I have sinned . . . " Kennedy says no modern boy would have said that. He would have said his trouble was his father's fault for being too strict or his mother's fault for making him go to church so much or . . .

"What a shocker to hear a boy stand up and say, 'I am to blame. The fault is mine.' But," Kennedy concludes, "this just might be the secret of his healing . . . . There can be no salvation for us until we accept our own responsibility."

Alfred Adler, the great pioneer psychologist, says essentially the same thing. He says we are not controlled by irresistible forces outside ourselves. When we are angry, he says, it is our own decision to be angry. We often feel justified to go into a real tirade because of all the injustices done to us. Even so, the emotions we call anger, the flood of temper, and the irresistible tirade come a moment later, Dr. Adler says, to support our decision that we have a right to be angry.

Think about that for a moment. If Adler is right, we are responsible for our anger, jealousies, hates, and even our love. In other words, someone or something else does not turn us on. WE TURN OURSELVES ON! One psychiatrist said to me, "50% of all illness is entirely emotional in origin, and of the other 50%, emotions are contributing factors." So, we have a responsibility for ourselves.

When Jesus asked the man at the Pool of Bethzatha, "Do you WANT to be well?" he went right to the heart of the problem. The sick man had been by the pool for 38 years, which really is making a career of a weakness. It was not a bad life. His friends brought him there in the morning and came for him at night. The city provided shade from the sun and protection from the rain under the five porches. He met his cronies there, and they talked together throughout the day. They watched others going about their work, which always is a pleasant recreation.

After all those years, in honesty, the man was not very anxious to change. So when Jesus asked, "Do you want to be well?" he saw right through the man.

Now, wait a minute! Does anyone really WANT to have problems? Does anyone want lung cancer? What a foolish question. But we want the things that produce it. Does anyone want to be an alcoholic? But we want the things that produce it. Do we really want this affair we are having? Probably. So Jesus' question, "Do you want to be different than you are?" goes right to the point. Until we are honest in answering it, nobody can do much for us.

At Massachusetts General Hospital in Boston, Dr. Erick Lindemann and his colleagues have learned something about human response to bereavement. His study began at the time of the catastrophic Coconut Grove fire in Boston years ago, when many survivors of that fire were brought to Mass General. Dr. Lindemann soon began to see that some of the burns were healing normally, but there were others that were not. To find the reasons, he examined the attitudes of those who were making rapid medical progress. They were facing up to their losses or the deaths of their loved ones. Even so, they were able to consider remaking their lives in the new situation.

Those whose burns healed slowly had very different responses. Some were resentful or rebellious. Others were stricken with guilt. All who were healing slowly had one thing in common: they could not face reality! They could not face the implications of their loss.

Do you want to be well?

At the Pool of Bethzatha, Jesus finally said to the sick man, "Get up. Fold your chair and walk." Do something. Make an effort. Here we get into difficulty, though, for certainly not everyone who tries gets well. Not everyone who prays solves his problems. But a lot more of them do than those who do not make an effort!

Many times I have heard surgeons say, "We do the surgery, but God does the healing." That is true. God does the healing. Sometimes, though, we can block God with our own lack of response to him. Protest and resentment can keep God at a distance.

Catherine Marshall observed during a long illness that day after day she was incapacitated by protest. She prayed for healing and was exasperated when God did not answer her prayers. It was not fair. She had a family to look after and work to do. She kept herself in a state of exhaustion with her protests. Finally, she said she gave up and prayed in humility, "Dear God, use me any way you please." Curiously, at the moment she ceased to protest, her healing began. She opened the door to God's power.

George Fox, the founder of the Quaker church, once described a woman who had been ill for a long time. She was resentful and felt that God had wronged her. Evidently Fox knew her very well, because when she recovered he commented, "God settled her mind, and she mended."

Today we may never be completely problem free in our attitudes, in our bodies or in our mental processes, but with God's help, we can be better than we are!

Do you WANT to be?

###

CHAPTER 15

My Huckleberry Christ

THE POWER TO RESIST

I was driving along in the car listening to the radio, and an old song I liked came on the radio. It was *Moon River*, from the movie *Breakfast At Tiffany's*. The song was already into the second verse.

> Two drifters
> Off to see the world.
> There's such a lot of world to see.
> We're after the same rainbow's end
> Waitin' 'round the bend—
> My Huckleberry friend,
> Moon River and me.

Those last two lines have always intrigued me: "My Huckleberry friend . . ." Huckleberry friend? Didn't that have something to do with Huckleberry Finn and his raft ride down the Mississippi with his friend, Jim, the runaway slave?

I went to the library and borrowed Mark Twain's novel, *The Adventures Of Huckleberry Finn* written in 1861 about boys growing up in the Mississippi Valley in the mid 19th century. Here's how Huck Finn begins,

You don't know about me, without you have read a book by the name of *The Adventures Of Tom Sawyer*, but that ain't no matter.

That book was made by Mr. Mark Twain, and he told the truth, mainly. There was things which he stretched, but mainly he told the truth [about] Aunt Polly, or the widow, or maybe Mary, and the Widow Douglas. It's mostly a true book; with some stretchers, as I said before.

There is one scene in the book about how Huck stopped praying:

Miss Watson she took me into the closet and prayed, but nothin' come of it. She told me to pray every day, and whatever I asked for I would get it. But it warn't so. I tried it. Once I got a fish line, but no hooks. It warn't any good to me without hooks. I tried for hooks three or four times, but somehow I couldn't make it work.

By and by, one day I asked Miss Watson to try for me, but she said I was a fool. She never told me why . . . . I said to myself, if a body can get anything they prays for, why don't Deacon Winn get back the money he lost . . . ? Why can't the widow Jones get back the silver snuff box that was stole? Why can't Miss Watson fat up? No, I says to myself, there ain't nothin' to it.

Huckleberry Christ? Didn't Jesus pray? Of course he did. But he also railed at the way people tried to pray. He told a story about a Pharisee and a tax collector who went into the Temple to pray (see chapter 13). The Pharisee was all full of his self righteousness, but the tax collector bowed his head and prayed, "Lord, be merciful to me, a sinner." Jesus said the tax collector went away from the Temple justified in the sight of God, but the Pharisee did not.

Then there was that scene with Tom Sawyer. Tom was always dreaming that he was someone important. Of course, he was not really. Aunt Polly saw to that, but in his daydreams, he was. He was the great general returning from the wars, riding his great charger, with the whole town turned out to cheer him. And there stood Becky Thatcher, with her lovely curls and soft eyes, worshipping her hero. And Aunt Polly, too, repenting that she had treated him so cruelly. He had shown the world they had misunderstood him, and now Tom Sawyer was enjoying his moment of triumph.

Then we grow up . . . but we still have that feeling. We never quite grow out of it. Why do we want to play the piano or paint pictures or even preach sermons? To help people, of course, but that is not the full reason.

We would be surprised, if we could analyze ourselves objectively, how much of this desire to be important enters everything we do. We like to do something good, but we also like to be praised for it. Alfred Adler, one of the pioneers of modern psychology, knew about that. He said this desire to be significant is the DOMINANT impulse in human nature, even stronger than sex.

Jesus knew about that centuries ago, when he chose his disciples in ancient Palestine. These disciples were ambitious men. They wanted to get ahead in the world, even ahead of each other. Two of them once came to Jesus and said, "Grant us, when you come into your glory, that the two of us may sit, one on the right hand and the other on the left." Isn't that amazing? That was James and John speaking. We call them "saints" today.

Jesus never feared their ambition. He only wanted to guide their ambition into worthy channels.

Most of you realize *The Adventures Of Huckleberry Finn* has been recognized as one of the half dozen or so most significant works of American literature. In fact, many critics rank it among the masterpieces of WORLD literature. It is a myth, a symbolic projection of all our hopes, values, fears, and aspirations.

Huck Finn is a wanderer. He is idealistic but also rational. He wants something more substantial than a materialistic society. He is sensitive, troubled by the way people treat people, but he still has a practical, realistic outlook. At times, he is a dreamer. As Mark Twain tells it, Huck and black Jim are floating down the Big River. "Once or twice of a night we would see a steamboat slipping along in the dark, and now and then she would belch a whole world of sparks up out of her chimneys, and they would rain down in the river and look awful pretty; then she would turn a corner . . . and leave the river still again."

One of the great scenes in the book, I think, is when Huck and Jim are with a couple scoundrels who are trying to sell Jim back into slavery. They have escaped from the two men but got separated in the process. Huck is trying to find Jim, and says,

Pretty soon I went out on the road, trying to think what I better do, and I run across a boy walkin,' and asked him if he's seen a strange black man dressed so and so, and he says,

"Yes."

"Whereabouts?"

"Down to Silas Phelps' place, two mile below here. He's a runaway . . . and they've got him. There's a $200 reward on him. It's like pickin' up money out'n the road."

In the culture of that era in the mid 1800s, it was considered the "right" thing to do to turn in a runaway slave. Huck was wrestling with his conscience. "It made me shiver, and I about made up my mind to pray . . . so I kneeled down. But the words wouldn't come. I knowed very well why they wouldn't come. It was because my heart warn't right; it was because I warn't square . . . I was playin' double."

Now, there is a strange twist to the story here, because Huck thought it was the "right" thing to turn Jim in. So he got a piece of paper and pencil and sat down and wrote, "Miss Watson, your runaway slave Jim is down here two mile below Pikesville, and Mr. Phelps has got him and will give him up for the reward if you send it."

But then, according to the story, he

> . . . got to thinkin' over our trip down the river; and I see Jim before me . . . in the day, and in the nighttime, sometimes moonlight, sometimes storms, and we a floatin' along, talkin,' and singin,' and laughin' . . . . I'd see him standing my watch on top of his'n, stead of callin' me, so I could go on sleepin,' and see how glad he was when I came back out of the fog . . . up there where the feud was . . . and I happened to look around and see that paper to Miss Watson about squealin' on Jim.

> I took it up, and held it in my hand. I was a-tremblin,' because I'd got to decide forever betwixt two things, and I knowed it. I studied a minute, sort of holding my breath, and then says to myself, "All right, then, I'll go to hell"—and tore up the paper! It was an awful thought, and awful words, but they was said. And I let them be said . . .

Centuries ago, Galileo said it. He rebelled against the established religion of his day about what was right. Copernicus rebelled, and so did Martin Luther. They said that the church was wrong. The church said they would go to hell, and they each replied, "All right, I'll go to hell! Here I stand," Martin Luther said. "I can do no other."

Jesus, too, said the leaders were wrong, and they crucified him.

Some time ago, a man told me that a friend of his reminded him of Christ.

"Which side of Christ?" I asked.

"What do you mean, which side?"

"Well, what was your friend like?"

"Oh, he was gentle and compassionate, never raised his voice. He liked kids, and even though he was in business he spent lots of time doing good—you know, like Jesus."

"That's what I meant when I asked which side of Jesus your friend was like," I said. "Jesus had another side entirely. Sometimes he was stern, formidable. Sometimes he DID raise his voice, became angry, and instead of comforting people, he said some mighty uncomfortable words."

When a person has two different sides, we try to remember the gentle one and forget the prickly side. At Christmas, we enjoy the sentimental story about the boy in the manger, but we ignore the part about King Herod killing the baby boys as he tried to eliminate Jesus (see Chapter 2). We like to hear about Jesus taking little children on his lap, as he looked out over the blue waters of the Galilee, but we neglect the other side of Jesus.

At first, Jesus was greeted with a great wave of popular enthusiasm, but he ran into increasing conflict with the religious leaders of his day: scribes, Pharisees, and Sadducees—the Establishment! Matthew tells us that at one time Jesus retaliated against these leaders and called them, "Whitewashed tombs!"

Imagine that. "Outwardly you appear beautiful," he said, "but inwardly you are full of dead people's bones." There men he was talking to ran the political, social, and religious life of the country.

> You blind guides, you try to strain a gnat out of your food, but you swallow a camel whole in one gulp . . . . You hypocrites, you wash the outside of the cup very carefully, but you leave the inside dirty . . . . You snakes, how can you escape damnation?

Who were these persons who opposed Jesus so bitterly? They were the scribes and Pharisees and Sadducees, the very best people of their day. They believed that every syllable, every letter of the law was holy. Take the matter of observing the Sabbath. The Old Testament said simply, "Remember the Sabbath day to keep it holy," and it goes on to say there must be no work on the Sabbath. They were convinced Jesus was breaking the Sabbath—and he was!

There was the matter of the disciples passing through a grain field one Sabbath afternoon, and they were hungry. They plucked a few grains, rubbed them together in their hands to get rid of the hulls, and ate them. The spies of the Pharisees were there and found Jesus and his disciples guilty on three counts: plucking the grain technically was reaping on the Sabbath, rubbing the grain in their palms was grinding, and the whole process was preparing food. Guilty.

Healing on the Sabbath was work and was, therefore, forbidden. So the Pharisees watched to see if Jesus would heal on the Sabbath. Jesus declared war! Defiantly, he healed a woman who could not stand up straight. He healed a man with dropsy and another who was born blind—all on the Sabbath.

You see, there is a difficult, prickly, huckleberry side to Christ. If Jesus was no more than a gentle teacher who went about doing good, I wonder why they bothered to crucify him. "If anyone would come after me, let him deny himself . . . . If anyone would ask you to go one mile with him, go with him two . . . . Love your enemies and pray for those who persecute you." Jesus said all that.

The person who sits back in his easy chair usually is blind to one of the most terrible facts of our day, the fact that Christians are at war. We are not Christians to come to terms with the world. We are here to change it! That is hard for moderns to hear, because we have paid little attention to this other side of Jesus, the huckleberry, sticky, prickly side.

Thank God, though, there is still another side to Jesus, and that is the dancing, friendly, kind of wild, joyous side of Jesus. There is a book by Kristen Ingram that brings this out. It's entitled *A Spiritual Journey With The Huckleberry Christ*. She writes:

> I longed for joy when I was a confused, depressed young mother, struggling to clean the house that seemed to hover over me, hostile. Sometimes I took college classes or gave piano lessons . . . . I was always looking for God, or rather for "Something More" that God had for me. I looked in all kinds of places: grand, empty cathedrals, silent forests, and dim corners. I read dusty books and went to meetings of vague people who said they had "An Answer."

> Therefore, it was to my utter and complete astonishment that I found God, and found my joy complete. One day I was reading my Bible and idly thought, "God, I want what it tells about there." Nothing happened that I could detect, but a few weeks later I found my joy in, of all places, a full church, with a badly played organ, birthday pennies bouncing on the floor, and children shuffling restlessly. God was there . . . in the same liturgy . . . in the same prayers . . . but

suddenly he jumped out from between the rubrics, looked at me and said, "Let's dance!"

My grandson, Andrew, is two years old. Andrew and I danced that afternoon in the backyard, and I know Christ danced with us. I wonder when Andrew will stop dancing with me. Now he is two. His cheeks are apricot and his hair is corn-colored and he is willing to dance with me under the filbert trees while I sing. How long will it be until he is horrified, or embarrassed at the sight of his crazy grandmother dancing like a blond bear with Christ?

"Grannuther!" he cried, "I think I saw Jesus dancing, too."

So it's a myth, is it, my Huckleberry Christ? But if it is, it's something that's universal, because it has all our hopes, values, fears, and aspirations. It has the prickly, the sticky, and the difficult, but also the dancing, friendly, and joyous side of Christ.

###

CHAPTER 16

The Sin of Boredom

"LIFE IS A PROFOUND AND PASSIONATE THING . . . "

A Chicago clergyman sat in the downtown office of a physician friend. As the muffled noise of traffic and L trains below floated through the closed windows, the doctor said, "The most deadly of human diseases is one which we can't touch with a knife or save people from with drugs."

"You mean cancer?"

"No, we'll get cancer yet. I mean boredom. There's more real wretchedness or torment driving people to folly—or what you parsons call sin—due to boredom than to anything else."

Now, all of us know something about boredom: the drudgery of doing the same thing over and over. The postman delivering the same mail, the receptionist simpering professionally at each patient, the mother getting the children off to school at the same hour, washing the same dishes, and sweeping the same floors. We all know about that.

And yet, boredom and monotony are not the same things. There are postmen who deliver mail and enjoy talking with people they meet. There are receptionists who like putting patients at ease. There are mothers who find a challenge in being mothers. These people are not bored. Bored people are empty people, people with nothing to live for, people with nothing outside themselves to serve.

A man was talking with me, and he said, "I have everything a person could reasonably want out of life. I'm head of my business and I have a fine home with a swimming pool, four cars and a boat but I've gotten to the place where I just don't give a damn."

The question for much of our culture is this: how can we take the risks out of life, make it more comfortable, and still escape the penalties of boredom? So people become heavy drinkers or juvenile delinquents or senile delinquents to fill the emptiness. As someone said, "We are fed up at 15 and fagged out at 40, and our idea of roughing it is turning down the dial on the electric blanket to low."

Oh, certainly that isn't true with all of us, but it is accurate for an amazing number. I am convinced the great danger of our day, with no great cause to lift us to our feet and no great God to believe in, is that the hunger will turn inward or become destructive. Certainly one of the reasons people turn to violence is because of boredom. One of the reasons people turn to drugs is boredom.

We all are aware today that alcohol is a narcotic, but sometimes action becomes a drug, a narcotic to deaden the pain of thought. Frequently, a nervous breakdown is preceded by furious action, something to make the mind forget. Amusements can become a drug. Its very name betrays its purpose: a-musing, not musing, not thinking, and millions try to fill the emptiness with it.

In fact, I am convinced war gets its rise, in part, from the torment of boredom. Clifton Fadiman once said, "The Crusades were stimulated in part by love of God, in part by love of loot, and in part by the terrible tedium of daily life."

One reason people periodically become terrorists or suicide bombers is because of emptiness. Once in Germany, I was talking with a woman who had escaped the Nazis during World War II. She described the effect Hitler had on German young people. So many of the youth had lost their sense of belonging. She said, "They don't count, so Hitler told them, 'No one loves you. I love you. No one will give you work. I will give you work. No one wants you. I want you.' And when they saw the sunlight in his eyes, they dropped their tools and followed Hitler."

C. S. Lewis, the late great Oxford don, suggests, "We often behave as though the Gospel is for someone else: the little, low, timid, warped, thin-blooded lonely people, or the passionate, sensuous, neurotic people. But it would be good to remember that 'nice' people sometimes get lost, too. We can be lost in all the old familiar ways: lost in pride, in self satisfaction, in irritability, in lust, or in just plain boredom. Then all of a sudden something happens. A great light shines for us. In a great love we fulfill ourselves. In the pursuit of an ideal we find our freedom. In some fire of forgiveness . . . or in some consuming sorrow we feel our hearts warmed by love."

While he was here on earth, Jesus met many bored people and cured them. One of these was the Samaritan woman he met at Jacob's Well. Jesus was on his way north to Galilee and had to pass through a segregated part of the country called Samaria. Jews had no dealings at all with Samaritans, because during one of the exiles, some of the Israelites remained in Israel and intermarried with the Canaanites.

When the Jews returned to their native soil, they wouldn't have anything to do with these half-Jews, half-Canaanites called Samaritans. Then Jesus met a Samaritan woman at Jacob's Well.

It was the middle of the day, and Jesus was hot, tired, and thirsty. Jesus had no bucket to draw water, so he asked this woman if she would give him a drink. She was incredulous: "How is it that you, a Jew, ask a drink of me, a woman of Samaria?"

She had had a boring life, which she tried to escape by marrying or living with a variety of men: six of them all together. All of them, though, left her more weary and bored than before.

Perhaps she felt like the wife recently who heard her husband was going to put an ad in *The Philadelphia Inquirer* telling everyone she had left him. She then inserted her own notice just beneath his. The first notice read:

> My wife, Mary, having left my bed and board, I will not be responsible for any of her debts. Signed, Henry Jones.

Directly following was her come-back:

> Very hard bed. Very little board. Awfully bored. Signed, Mary Jones.

The woman of Samaria and Mary Jones had the same trouble, although Mary had not tried as many times as the woman of Samaria. I wonder if part of their trouble was that they were not so much bored with their husbands as bored with themselves. The lack might have been on the inside.

In Arthur Miller's play *Death Of A Salesman*, the two sons of Willie Loman are talking.

> Biff says: "Are you content, Hap? You're a success, aren't you? Are you content?"

> "Hell, no!"

> "Why, you're making money, aren't you?"

"All I can do now is wait for the merchandise manager to die. And suppose I get to be merchandise manager. He's a good friend of mine, and he just built a terrific estate on Long Island . . . and now he's building another one. He can't enjoy it once it's finished. I know that's just what I'd do. I don't know what the hell I'm working for . . . . It's crazy. But then, it's what I always wanted: my own apartment, a car, plenty of money. But still, I'm bored."

The theologian Elton Trueblood said it is wrong to say the people of the world want peace instead of war. "Actually most of us like war better than we like peace," he said. "We like it because it saves us from boredom, mediocrity and dullness."

If that is true, then perhaps the greatest threat for the people of the world is not the men in Beijing or Cuba or Iraq or North Korea. Perhaps the greatest threat is from ordinary, common people like us: those who haven't found any tremendous reason for living. We become so fed up that unconsciously we give way to violent attitudes that lead to war.

I do not know whether Dr. Trueblood is right or not, but I do know that hot blood flows in the veins of humanity. It is God's gift to us. It is part of the image of God in us, something that refuses to be mediocre, something that makes us want to fill our souls with a life that will damn us, rather than nothing.

But if we have the consciousness that what we are doing adds up to an existence of eternal significance, life can take on luster, zest, and new meaning.

Some years ago, Aldous Huxley wrote a best seller entitled *Brave New World*. It pictures the world as science might be able to make it: without pain, struggle, discomfort, and effort. Even when a little discomfort does creep in, there is the drug "Soma" to take the rough edges off life. Near the end of the story a new character is introduced. I think he is the only worthy character in the novel. He is called a savage, though, and he comes from the outer fringes of civilization. He meets the Controller of the World, and the Controller explains the kind of society they have, then he adds, "Just in case somebody is taken by reverses we have Soma close at hand to give them a holiday from the troublesome facts."

But when the holiday is over, the same troublesome facts still are there, and the people of *Brave New World* are even less capable of facing reality.

Finally, the savage replies, "That's just like you, getting rid of everything unpleasant . . . . It's too easy. I don't want comfort, I want God. I want poetry. I want danger. I want freedom. I want goodness."

In nineteenth century America, Oliver Wendell Holmes was a physician, Harvard professor, writer, and popular lecturer. He said,

> "Through our great good fortune in our youth, our hearts were touched by fire. It was given to us to learn at the outset that life is a profound and passionate thing. While we are permitted to scorn nothing but indifference, and do not pretend to undervalue the worldly rewards of ambition, we have seen with our own eyes, beyond and above the gold fields, the snowy heights of honor."

To escape the sin of boredom, then, our hearts need to be touched with fire. We are to be participants not spectators in life, and we are to find something beyond ourselves to tie to.

###

CHAPTER 17

A New Kind of Freedom

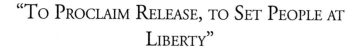

"To Proclaim Release, to Set People at Liberty"

It was 1787 in Philadelphia. After a sticky and stormy summer of arguing, our Constitutional Convention came forth with a document that began, "We the people of the United States, in order to form a more perfect union . . . and secure the blessings of liberty for ourselves and for our posterity do establish this constitution of the United States of America."

When the debaters finished their work and came out on the steps of Constitution Hall to read their document to the people, one little charwoman tugged at Benjamin Franklin's sleeve. She asked, "Is it a monarchy or a republic?" for that had been one of the most virulent debates of the summer. Franklin replied. "We have given you a republic . . . if you can keep it."

That was in 1787, but today those words are critical.

When women are given rights equal to men
it does not remove responsibility, it produces it.

When young people are given the freedom to buy drinks at a bar it does not remove responsibility, it produces it.
When workers are given the freedom to vote down a contract offered by the bosses, it does not remove responsibility, it produces it.
When blacks
and Hispanics
and gays
and Asians
and wise and unwise people
and shouting, angry people
are demanding rights we need to hear again the words,

"We have given you a republic . . . if you can keep it." Or the words of Berdyev, "People are slaves, because freedom is difficult, and slavery is easy."

I wonder how many of us have ever read the Declaration of Independence. It was signed July 4, 1776, but surveys indicate that only about one-fourth of us have read it. So it shocks us to discover that the basic premise on which the declaration stands is a RELIGIOUS appeal. It appeals to the "Supreme Judge of the world," and the truths that it says are self-evident are because our founders felt Almighty God had established them.

This simple idea of personal freedom is founded on the Christian idea of God and the sacredness of life. That is strange to us today. However, it released in American life a driving force that created social progress and achievements unknown before in the history of humankind.

You see, we need to be reminded that the basic idea of Christ is NOT TO BIND US, BUT TO SET US FREE.

When Jesus preached his first sermon in his home synagogue of Nazareth, he said, "The spirit of the Lord has anointed me . . . to proclaim release to the captives . . . to set at liberty those who have been bruised" (isn't that all of us?). Every time I think of that passage, I am aware that Jesus isn't just giving us beautiful ideals. He is telling us the law of life itself. It is a NEW KIND OF FREEDOM!

Certainly we have all kinds of ideas buzzing around inside us: "I'd be free if I hadn't been married (or unmarried). I'd be free if I had a new house . . . if I could do more traveling . . . if I didn't have to work so hard." But freedom is not necessarily a better marriage or a new house or more travel or less hard work. Oh, sure, sometimes those things do help.

I have a friend who has made many millions of dollars, and certainly her style of life is different from what it would have been if she had never left the Ozarks. Yet once she said, "There are just so many steaks you can eat, there are just so many houses you can live in, or beds you can sleep in." So she is still working, because that is the way she is most free.

Happiness might be produced by a better marriage or a new house or fame . . . . But freedom really is WHAT WE FEEL INSIDE US ABOUT THE THINGS THAT HAPPEN TO US.

One minister went to a church conference in Tennessee and said to himself, "I came to this conference feeling I was serving the coldest church in the coldest denomination in Christendom. I was complaining to God about it just this morning in my prayers, and God said to me, 'Oh, John, I'm so sorry for you and the situation you're in. But if I can thaw YOU out, and make YOU a loving, honest, and real person, maybe I can change your church and part of your denomination through you.'"

In that great scene where Jesus read the scripture in his home synagogue, the passage he chose was from Isaiah, "God sent me to proclaim release, to set people at liberty . . . ." Not to be a moral policeman, not to be a parent figure to all the world, but TO SET PEOPLE FREE! Maybe that is what the Christian faith is all about: not so much making rules and restrictions and regulations. The Pharisees did that until the world was sick to death of them.

But Jesus came TO SET PEOPLE FREE.

One day we may discover that we have achieved a new kind of freedom, an emotional freedom that is greater than any we have known before: freedom from the urge to control others.

Did you know that the number one problem in marriage is control? Whether we are talking about money or sex or how to raise the kids, the main problem in marriage is control: "I know what's best for you. Why don't you do it MY way. I'm the only one who knows what's right around here."

There was a seminary president who told the story of when he was a student years ago in Chicago's inner city. He said he had an experience that still makes him feel ashamed:

> One night as I was about to go to bed, there was a loud crash outside my window. A car had careened up on the sidewalk and hit a fireplug. People had spilled out in all directions. I sensed this was a chance to help and I dashed out into the night, ready to take care of the victims. The first one I found was a large, middle-aged woman. She asked to sit down, but instead of easing her to the sidewalk, which would have made sense, I offered to open the church and get her comfortable on a couch off the sanctuary.
>
> In my unwise enthusiasm to help I had not reckoned with the distance she would have to be dragged, or the steps she would have to climb. It was a nightmare. When the police ambulance arrived a few minutes later, I had the poor moaning lady jammed into an opera chair, from which the police extricated her only with great difficulty and understandable profanity.
>
> If I only had ended it there, but I have proceeded through my life assuming that I knew what was best for people. I have seen myself bending down over the spiritually bruised and

bleeding, trying to help them, but always I assumed I knew what was best for them.

Couldn't it just be that Christianity is not so much helping people as enabling them to find freedom?

Having said that, we also must stress that FREEDOM DOES HAVE RESPONSIBILITY. Dr. Robert A. Fitch, professor of ethics at the Pacific School of Religion in Berkeley, California, was reviewing some of the great societies of the past. "Athens was one," he said, "and Renaissance England was another. We also must include the American colonies at the time of the American Revolution."

Then a student asked Dr. Fitch. "Well, what makes a society great?"

"Creativity," the professor answered. "A society is great when it is creating something significant."

"Such as?"

"There are three things which result in greatness," Dr. Fitch continued. "An air of freedom, an air of adventure, and a climate of faith."

"Do you think we have those today?"

"If we do, they also are accompanied by a growing caricature of liberty, a personal freedom without any sense of responsibility. It's a kind of individualistic liberty which can destroy itself."

Perhaps we need to be reminded that one of his biographers said of Lincoln, "We find it momentous that Lincoln used the word 'responsibility' nearly as often as he used the word 'liberty.'"

A new kind of freedom also might include BEING RELEASED FROM GLOOMINESS AND HATE. One summer I met a radiant woman, and I asked her how she came to be that way. She said that several years ago someone asked her, "Does the world need another person like you?" She confessed that at the time she was the gloomiest, sourest, most negative person imaginable. She did not want to be that kind of person, so she freed herself of her gloomy, sour, negative thoughts. Now she communicates love, power, and joy. Freedom in Christ.

I once heard a Korean young man named Koo Yong Na tell how his father was killed during the Korean War. Mr. Koo said,

> He was not killed by a communist, but by an American soldier. My father was selling American cigarettes and had only one carton left. There was a Korean who wanted to buy the cigarettes, when an American soldier came up and tried to take them. My father couldn't speak English, but he tried to say that the Korean was there first.

> The American soldier pulled out his pistol and shot my father, took the cigarettes and walked away. I remember falling to the ground beside my father, not feeling anything, sobbing, calling to my father who didn't respond. He was dead.

Eventually Mr. Koo came to America and he said,
> You can imagine how hard it was for me to come to America, to face Americans, after an American had killed my father.

> The American soldier eventually was brought to trial. Killing a Korean civilian during wartime was a crime punishable by death. They asked my mother, who was a Christian, what punishment should be given and she replied. "Give him the lightest possible punishment. It wasn't the soldier who killed my husband. It was war."

It is interesting to note that 1885 was when the first Christian missionaries arrived in Korea, but now almost a century and a quarter later, 25% of the population of Korea are Christian, and Koo Yong Na is a Christian minister serving in the state of New Jersey.

So in Christ we CAN be free, free from hate, free to love, free to be honest, free to change, and free to be responsible so that the love and power and joy of Christ will radiate from us.

###

CHAPTER 18

Fret Not Thy Gizzard Out!

THE POWER TO FIND PEACE

Many articles have been written about tension and stress, and we are alarmed by elaborate graphs showing diminishing life expectancy because of stress. It is true, stress can make us sick. We are told about the illnesses from which we can suffer because of our inability to cope with tension. We are supposed to relax, slow down before we break down, do less and live longer, stay out of stress producing situations, avoid stressful people, take more vacations, have more fun, sit in a hot tub, cry more, get more exercise, and on and on and on.

There was an elderly grandfather who, at family gatherings when people were telling how stressed they were, would piously quote what he claimed was his favorite Bible verse, "Fret not thy gizzard out."

Frequently someone would remind him there is no such verse in the Bible, to which he would answer, "Well, there oughta be!" The old man was close to the thinking of our Lord, however, despite the fact that people do not have gizzards. Jesus once said (Matthew 6 and Luke 12), "Don't be anxious about food or clothing, for life is more than food, and the body more than clothing." Then Jesus told about the anemones, which blazed their color over the fields, pastures, and even the ditches of Palestine. King Solomon in all his finery, Jesus said, was not as impressive.

Stress is an enormous problem for many. Living on a fast track need not cause stress, although it can. Certainly, if stress is constant, it can turn toxic and break down the body. However, even when stress is massive, repetitive, or chronic, it does not automatically lead to illness. There are people who handle immense responsibilities at home, at work, in church, and community activities and do them with amazing effectiveness and ease.

It may be that our biggest problem is learning how to make tension work FOR us, rather than against us.

Duke University Medical Center made a study of the link between Type A behavior and heart disease. Type A is the hard-driving, competitive person, and it had been thought that these people would develop coronary and blood pressure problems more than average persons. Instead, they found that not all Type A people are alike. Some are healthier than the national average. They thrive on competition and challenge.

Other Type A persons, however, have a negative view of their situations. These Type As are tense and apprehensive and think most of the people near them are liars and cheats. They DID develop heart problems.

I am convinced that it is not necessarily how hard we work that causes tension. There are, in fact, two types of stress: good, creative stress and distress! Many have learned how to employ their stress coping mechanisms to work for them. The problem is not how much we do but in the goals, attitudes, and resources with which we do it. It is how we do what we do!

The *Wall Street Journal* reported a study by behavioral scientists at the University of Chicago about executives which would result in a large number of promotions and demotions. They were worried about the stress it would cause their executives.

The study found distinct differences in the executives: some became ill from high blood pressure, ulcers, stomach and muscle problems, and colds. Some, though, remained healthy! Those who stayed healthy, the researchers said, had a sense of commitment that involved their whole life, not just their work.

Right here I would like to suggest a revolutionary thought: TENSION ACTUALLY IS A DESIRABLE THING IN LIFE. In fact, we need tension. We need a new kind of tension, a saving, creative tension in our lives.

There was an interview in *U.S. News And World Report* with Dr. Roy W. Menninger, the president of the Menninger Foundation in Topeka, Kansas. He says, "I'm convinced that stress does not need to be bad for people. If we weren't stressed and distressed by the challenges of our world, then nothing would get done. A lot of people," he says, "thrive on stress, particularly executives. Take it away and their jobs become boring."

This approach to tension can be grounded in belief in God. Exercise, certainly, eat properly, yes, think pleasant thoughts, sit in a hot tub, whatever works, but do not stop there. Put yourself in the way of the great restoring energies of God. Dr. Herbert Benson, a Harvard cardiologist, says in a recent book that belief in God is in itself beneficial to health. God can make you less tense and apprehensive and easier to live with. And as I stated in chapter 5, Carl Jung, the great Swiss psychiatrist, has written, "I have never been able to affect a lasting cure in any of my patients until the patient has discovered a creative faith in God."

Remember that the world into which Jesus came was not any more peaceful than ours. At Bethlehem, the angels sang, "Peace on earth, goodwill . . . ," but King Herod's soldiers were killing all the two-year-old baby boys as they hunted for Jesus. Peaceful?

Later, as Jesus and his disciples finished their last meal together and knowing that he faced a cross, Jesus said to them, "Peace I give you, my peace I leave with you, NOT AS THE WORLD GIVES, give I unto you."

They did crucify Jesus, but it was not because he talked about the birds soaring through the air or wildflowers covering the hillsides. They crucified Jesus because he, fully knowing the consequences, confronted the priests and religious leaders who were making themselves comfortable at the expense of the poor. Jesus wanted to change all that because he said it was not religion. So they crucified him.

Close your eyes for a moment and listen to the sounds you may hear. There is the sound of an automobile outside, the hum of a heater or air conditioner, an airplane flying overhead, a dishwasher finishing a cycle. These are creative tensions that perform useful functions in our society. People who do not have a creative tension in their lives, the caring, the sense of a deadline, the race to complete a project, really may have no real life!

Some think a person has only limited strength, but that isn't always so. I read about a man who was frightened by a large Dalmatian dog and cleared a wall, which he later measured. The wall was six feet three inches tall, and until that time, the man never had been able to jump more than five feet. All of us know how much extra strength we have when the kids are sick or a husband or wife is in the hospital and we are needed.

You have read that Abraham Lincoln and Edwin Stanton lived in the same world, under the same pressures, stresses, and strains. Yet, whatever happened outwardly, Lincoln remained quiet inwardly. On the other hand, Stanton, if he wasn't upset all the time, was ready to be upset at a moment's notice.

Whether we like it or not, there is stress in life. Yet, consider this: there also is stress caused by a dull, unadventurous life! It is caused by stifling the strength and energy the Lord has given us, and we become dull, unexciting, stressful people.

There is a book entitled *The Joy Of Stress*. Imagine, the JOY of stress! It is written by a Canadian medical doctor named Peter G. Hanson. He says many people with sedate working lives "actively seek stress in the form of parachuting, cliff climbing, skiing or horror movies. Such stresses bring more joy into their lives. Too much stress," he says, "can become a negative force [but] too little stress can be just as dangerous . . . unless new stresses and interests can be found. Extra responsibilities will add needed stress, and can improve your overall efficiency and happiness dramatically."

This also is true for children. At a workshop in the Nebraska Psychiatric Institute in Omaha, Dr. Frank Main was discussing responsibility among family members and said, "Children need the opportunity to overcome adversity. In fact, they need the opportunity to overcome adversity even more than they need tender, loving care."

Years ago I was a Navy chaplain in the Pacific. Our ship went through a hurricane near the Van Dieman Strait as we were sailing from Japan into the China Sea. I was in the radio shack four decks up, and I watched the hurricane through a porthole. I could see the wind whipping the water and waves breaking over us above the fourth deck. I could feel the ship shudder, as the propeller was lifted out of the water by the storm, and I could hear the clanging of loose gear below. Then suddenly we sailed into the heart of the storm.

I had heard there was a calm at the center of a hurricane, but until then I thought it was just a phrase, a relative calm. Then the sun came out. There were a few scattered clouds and no breeze at all. We were in the middle of a magnificent sunny day, at the heart of a hurricane.

Now hear this: the peace that God gives does not set us apart from the tumult but at the heart of it. In the center of a mad world, Jesus speaks again to us, in our day, "Peace I give you, my peace I leave with you, not as the world gives, give I unto you." We stand with God with inner serenity and peace.

###

CHAPTER 19

Even with Problems, You Can Be Happy!

THE POWER TO FIND JOY

Christianity is a joyful religion. Even as Jesus was facing his cross, he said to his disciples, as they were having their last meal together, "These things I have spoken to you, that my joy may be in you, and that your joy may be full (John 15:11)." Earlier Jesus began his Sermon on the Mount with nine ways to be happy. We call them "beatitudes," or as one author terms it, "The Be-Happy Attitudes."

It may be surprising to some, in fact, that religion can be joyous. Matthew says, "When you pray, do not look gloomy." In the first century, there was singing and dancing along with the prayers and blessings.

The movie, *The Chosen,* is the story of two Jewish boys growing up in Brooklyn. One is an orthodox Hassidic Jew, and the other is a Reformed or liberal Jew. Many non Jews were startled in viewing the film to see the Hassidic Jews with their long black coats, their flat black hats, and the long side curls dancing, drinking wine, and walking upside down on their hands as part of a Hassidic wedding celebration.

For decades, psychologists have been doing research on depression, but only recently have they begun actively studying what makes us happy. It is called "positive psychology." Martin Seligman, a psychology professor at the University of Pennsylvania, is termed the father of positive psychology. He believes an optimistic outlook is the key to happiness and that IT CAN BE LEARNED! He has spent 30 years in research on the topic, and his results are in his book, *Learned Optimism*. He says that optimistic people tend to minimize the causes of their misfortune and instead take credit for the good things. On the other hand, pessimists blame themselves for their misfortune and believe that good events are only chance.

Now, of course, we must not get the idea that happiness means constant ecstasy. "If people seek ecstasy much of the time," says psychologist Ed Diener of the University of Illinois, "they are likely to be disappointed. Happy people," he says, "report mild-to-moderate pleasant emotions most of the time, rather than intense positive moments some of the time."

You see, we can refuse to get stuck in our own problems. There is a wonderful woman who has traveled with my wife and me. She is always on the tour bus on time, is cheerful, and even though she has been almost everywhere, is interested in what we are seeing.

Now, Alyce is in her eighties, and people in their eighties have problems just because they are in their eighties. One day I was sitting beside her, and I asked, "Alyce, when did you take your happy pill?" She paused a moment, then said,

> You know, it was a decision I made a long time ago. I just decided I was going to be happy, just like that! When my husband and I were young and went on our first tour, there was a couple in the group who complained about everything. "Oh, that was an awful meal we had this noon. Isn't that an attractive hotel across the street? Why aren't we staying there,

instead of this place? I wish our room faced in the other direction, where the river is. Why is the driver going so slow?"

Well, I just got sick of listening to their constant complaining. I decided right then I wasn't going to be like that. And I haven't been. I suppose that was my "happy pill," as you call it, Dick.

Alyce was right. We can decide right now that even though we have problems—and all of us do—we are going to be happy about life. Remember that Jesus faced a cross, a CROSS, and still said, "These things I have spoken to you, that my joy may be in you, and that your joy may be full."

The question we must ask ourselves sometime is, "What is happiness?" We have so many definitions. Years ago I was Navy chaplain in the Pacific. Many of the men thought happiness was drinking six beers, ten beers, or more. One engineering officer said to me, "All I want when I go ashore is a jug and a jump."

One of the classics of literature is Goethe's play, *Faust*. Dr. Faust, the hero, was a middle-aged scholar and scientist who is honored and well educated, but he was afraid he would never know what it meant to be really alive. Dr. Faust made a bargain with the devil, giving the devil his soul in the hereafter in exchange for one moment so fulfilling he could say, "Let it be like this forever."

In one of his books, Rabbi Harold S. Kushner tells how Goethe began writing the story at 20, then set it aside for other things. He went back to it at 40 and completed it shortly before his death at age 83.

At the beginning of the play, Faust is middle-aged and wants to experience everything: wealth, power, travel, and the ability to make love to any woman he desires. Faust does it all, but no matter how much wealth he acquires or how many women he seduces, he still is not happy.

Now, of course, we are not like that. We do not have the dream of unlimited wealth or power or fame. We have decided to slow down. The old ticker just will not stand the fast track. We have decided to smell the flowers and not try anymore for the corner office with six windows on the top floor. We have decided to drive a Mitsubishi or Buick or Jeep, instead of a Cadillac. And we are still not happy?

The more counseling I do, the more I am convinced our happiness does not depend on outer circumstances. As one person expressed it, "Whether I drive a Mercedes or a clunker, it's possible to be joyful!" It is not if the stock market goes up or if I get a better job or if I buy a better house or if I get married or unmarried. Certainly our well being is affected by what happens to us. And yet, survey after survey has shown that many people without material advantages are surprisingly happy, and many with all the advantages are distressed.

Aleksandr Solzhenitsyn, the great Russian writer mentioned in chapter 3, was branded a traitor by the Russian state and was sent to a prison camp in the dreaded gulag of Siberia. After his release, he wrote a second book about his life in the gulag, which was permitted to be published. Solzhenitsyn said it was in prison camp when "I learned that a line between good and evil passes not between countries, not between political parties, not between classes, but down, straight down each separate, individual heart."

Maybe it would help to get outside ourselves, to take ourselves out of the center and put God there. Most of us find it difficult to change, or in fact, we do not WANT to change, even for the better. Psychologists call this homeostasis, staying the same, because it is scary trying to remake ourselves.

There is a minister who attended a conference in Texas and said,

I got to talking with a perky little white-haired woman who asked, with a glint in her eyes, "I bet you can't guess what I used to be." I didn't know what she was getting at, then she continued, "I used to be a professional gambler. Would you believe that once I risked over $100,000 on a single spin of the roulette wheel? It was in Vegas, and I was having the hottest streak of my career. When I went to the tables, I won two out of every three times I played. I really had it going. By 11:30 that night I had run my original $5,000 to $50,000, and by midnight I had $100,000.

"My husband wanted me to quit . I said no. I had this intuition about the next spin. I let everything ride, and I lost. I was sick for days. It was the biggest risk I had ever taken."

Then the motherly, white-haired woman laughed and said, "Since then I've taken an even bigger risk. I heard about God's love, and I bet everything I had on it. I stopped gambling. I said to my husband, 'Sam, don't laugh. I'm going to be a teacher down at the church.' I enrolled in seminary, took some Bible courses, and now I'm the head honcho! I direct the whole Christian education program."

It was the biggest risk she had ever taken. In fact, it is the greatest risk any of us ever take, to believe that God loves us. We should respond to that love with everything we are and have and then do something for God's other children.

You see, so many of us do not go far enough. We want to get ourselves feeling comfortable. We call it "integrated," which means our mind, body, and emotions are all working peacefully together. We are whole . . . aren't we?

One of the great pioneer psychiatrists was Dr. Roberto Assagiaoli, an Italian who said that we must go beyond the feeling good, the integration, the wholeness, and begin to ask, "Why? What's it for, this feeling good?" He called it a "synthesis," so that we are at harmony—not only within ourselves but also with other people and with God.

The Sun Cities are finding that, for many residents, golf and cocktail parties are not enough. As one woman said, "I feel very unproductive." So now the residents do volunteer work, take all kinds of classes to do worthwhile things, and even start small businesses. Many years ago, the great Harvard psychologist, William James, said, "The most important thing in life is to live your life for something more important than your life."

Back to the story of Dr. Faust. By the time we come to the end of the story, the author, Goethe, is in his 80s and his hero, Faust, has aged along with him. Instead of winning fights, attracting young women, sipping the finest wines, and sampling food from the world's best chefs, Faust now is at work building dikes to reclaim land from the sea where people can live and work, plant gardens, and help people work in them. For the first time, Faust now can say, "Let this moment linger. This . . . is . . . GOOD."

One of my favorite movies—in fact, it is on everyone's list of favorite movies—is *Casablanca*. The hero is Rick Blaine, played by Humphrey Bogart. Rick at first is a cynical, self-protecting person. He stays ahead by looking out only for himself.

The movie is set in Morocco, where Rick runs a bar during World War II. There are two phrases everyone remembers: Rick is having a drink with Ingrid Bergman and lifts his glass and says, "Here's looking at YOU, kid." The other one is when he says to the piano player in his bar, "Play it again, Sam."

Then a suspicious man is arrested by the Gestapo in Rick's bar, and he asks Rick, "Why didn't you help me?" Rick says, "I don't stick my neck out for anyone."

Rick knows he does not want to be like the Nazi officers in *Casablanca*, though: tough, powerful, and unsentimental. At the end of the movie, Rick gives up his chance for escape in a sacrificial act for the woman he loves, Ingrid Bergman, and is condemned to stay in north Africa.

Like Faust, Rick Blaine found life unlivable when he thought only of himself. As he saved others, he also saved himself. Your attitude really does have an affect on how things work out. Even when you cannot change your life, you still can change your attitude. When you do, your life changes . . . . You CAN be happy.

###

CHAPTER 20

Pure in Heart— What's That?

Putting It Together

Mark Twain, the author of *Huckleberry Finn*, sometimes began his lectures by introducing himself in the third person. He would say, "I don't know much about this man. I know only two things about him. One is, he's never been in the penitentiary, and the other is, I don't know why he hasn't!"

Whether or not we deserve to be in the penitentiary, most of us do have a slight suspicion that we are not pure in heart. Or that in this tough, competitive world we CAN'T be pure in heart. Or that we just do not WANT to be pure in heart.

A Sunday school teacher once asked her class how many wanted to be pure in heart. One little boy put up his hand, and the teacher asked, "Do you want to be pure in heart?" "Yes," he said, "and if I can't have that I'd like to have a liquid crystal TV in our house."

Pure in heart. Either we do not want it, or we do not understand it. In the Gospel according to Matthew, Jesus went up on the mountain, sat down, and began to tell the people what happiness means and how we can be happy. These sayings, which are an introduction to his Sermon on the Mount, have been called "beatitudes," but really they are happinesses that can exist here and now. Oh, I know that so much of the time we think of happiness as something we will find when our circumstances change. When we are promoted to vice president of the corporation, when we can go skiing in Colorado and escape civilization, or when we move to another house, then we will be happy.

Strangely, Jesus did not tell us about any of those things. One of the things he DID say was, "Happy are the pure in heart, for they shall see God." Today? In our world?

James Moffatt, the translator of the Bible, once said that this beatitude, or happiness, really should be translated, "Blessed are those who are not double minded, for they shall be admitted to the intimate presence of God."

Our lives are so fragmented. A business person has a report to prepare, the telephone keeps ringing, then he has to run to a meeting, discuss programs with the staff, write letters, and on and on and on. Your life is like that, and so is mine. BUT THAT'S NOT BEING DOUBLE MINDED. Being double minded is having two different goals in life, two entirely different value systems.

Edward S. Martin has a poem about double mindedness:

Within my earthly temple there's a crowd:
There's one of us that's humble, one that's proud.

There's one that's broken hearted for his sins,
There's one that, unrepentant, sits and grins.

There's one that loves his neighbor as himself,
And one that cares for naught but fame and pelf.

From such corroding care I should be free,
If I could once determine which is me!

Double mindedness.

Jesus had a great deal to say about double mindedness in his Sermon on the Mount. We do our religious acts with divided motives. We give to God, but also we want to be seen and appreciated by people. We try to lay up treasures in heaven, but more of them are stored on earth. We are anxious about God's kingdom but also about what we shall eat and drink and wear. Jesus said that these are some of the causes of failure. I didn't write that, Jesus said it.

There is another poem about a double minded centipede.

A centipede was happy quite, until a frog in fun
said, "Pray, which leg comes after which?"
This raised her mind to such a pitch,
she lay distracted in the ditch,
considering how to run.

Jesus said, "Happy are those who are not double-minded, for they shall be admitted to the intimate presence of God." There is another, slightly different, translation of this beatitude, or happiness, by J. B. Phillips. "Happy are those who are UTTERLY SINCERE, for they shall see God." Sincere, pure in heart?

The origin of the word "sincere," by the way, is in Latin, and it comes from two Latin words, *sine*, meaning without, and *cera*, meaning wax. Sincere, without wax.

The word grew out of an ancient practice of Roman furniture makers. In old Rome, the makers of furniture would fill cracks in the wood with transparent wax. Wax, of course, was not strong, but the furniture appeared to be perfect. They could touch up holes and cracks so that they would LOOK okay, until the purchaser got it home. To counter this practice, honest craftsmen would stamp their furniture, *Sine cera*, without wax. So Jesus, according to J. B. Phillips, says, "Happy are the utterly sincere, for they shall see God."

There is still another interpretation to this happiness, or beatitude, "Happy are the pure in heart." There is a Christian youth musical entitled *Lightshine*, which is about these beatitudes, or happinesses.

In it, there is a Mime who, of course, cannot talk. She has to act out everything or dance everything in pantomime. She goes to one of the boys and tries to ask him, "Teach me to be happy."

He misunderstands and says, "You want me to teach you to dance?"

"No, no, no!" she acts out. "To be HAPPY!"

"Oh, you want us to teach you to be happy! Well," he says, "we've got a system. You've got to have it here, in your heart. You've gotta have a pure heart." Then he realizes the Mime doesn't understand, so he says, "You gotta get your heart and your mind together. Yeah. You gotta get your motives and your mind together. You gotta get your heart and your head straight. Yeah. That's it. You gotta put it together if you wanta be happy."

Happy are those who put it together. Happy are those who are utterly sincere. Happy are those who are not double minded. That is what it means to be pure in heart. The pure in heart see God.

How do you see God?

Usually we see what we are trained to see. A tour group was going through the Louvre in Paris and saw some of the great paintings and sculptures of the world. At the end of the tour, the guide asked if there were any questions. One American woman wanted to know what kind of wax they used on the floors. She saw what she had been trained to see.

A psychologist brought a group of boys and girls into a room for two minutes, then took them out and asked them to make a list of things they had noted while they were there. The lists varied all the way from ten to forty objects. But not one young person noted a single thing that could not be seen with his or her eyes. In the room, noises were coming in from the street, the sound of a piano in another part of the building, the scent of a cigar—all of those had been purposely introduced, but no one caught them. Usually we see what we are trained to see.

Your daughter comes home to dinner and goes through the meal with what she thinks is her usual composure. She believes she is in perfect control, but across the table, mother detects some suppressed emotion and says, "Out with it, Mary. Something's bothering you." How do you see?

One man lives in a town and sees it negatively, critically. He sees the pettiness of the people and the stodginess of the place. Another person sees how friendly the people are, the job opportunities, and the good schools and churches. We see with our eyes . . . and our minds . . . and our whole beings!

Holman Hunt was working on his great painting, *The Light of the World*, depicting Jesus at night holding a lantern, knocking on a door that symbolized the door to our hearts. They say he spent three years, off and on, trying to get the right atmosphere for that painting. Trying to portray the wintry light of Christ's lantern, Hunt worked often at night in bitter cold. It took him three years to capture the right atmosphere.

Can we expect to see God in three minutes or, as James Moffatt translates it, to "be admitted into the intimate presence of God?"

A few years ago, there was an all black cast of George Gershwin's American folk opera, *Porgy And Bess*, touring Russia. Christmas Day found them in Leningrad. Eleven members of the cast attended services that morning in an evangelical Christian church, where the people, even though they were persecuted for their faith, still held services there.

Among those who attended the service on Christmas Day was Theda Boggs, who played the Strawberry Woman in the opera. She told of the service and mentioned how, as their visitors from

America left, the little congregation sang in Russian *God Be with You 'Til We Meet Again.*

As the Russian Christians stood, waving white handkerchiefs and singing, it was a moving experience. Afterward Theda Boggs sat in the lobby of the Astoria Hotel in Leningrad, and someone asked her why she was weeping. She said, "I'm all torn to pieces. I've been going to church ever since I could walk, but I never felt God like I felt Him today. Oh, honey, He was there."

So Jesus looks at us and says that seeing God depends on clearing away the rubbish, the garbage of the soul. Then we find freedom from duplicity, freedom from double motives, and we discover a liberty of living we never dreamed possible.

###

CHAPTER 21

No Sudden Saints

Neither Saints Nor Prostitutes Are Made Quickly

While driving near the east bank of the Jordan River a few years ago, some English tourists saw ten girls who were dressed in bright Arab robes. One was playing a fast rhythm on an Arab finger drum, and for a few minutes, they danced along in front of the car.

The guide said they were going to keep the bride company until her groom arrived. Someone asked if there was any chance of seeing the wedding, but he said, "No. No one knows for sure when it will be—maybe tonight, maybe tomorrow night. Who knows?" Then he went on to explain that because of ancient transportation methods in that area, the groom comes unexpectedly, sometimes in the middle of the night. When the groom is about to arrive, he sends a man along the street in advance shouting, "The bridegroom is coming. The bridegroom is coming!"

Back in the village, the bridal party must be ready to go out into the street and meet the groom whenever he arrives, even though it is late and the bridal party is napping. "In this area," the guide said, "no one is allowed in the streets after dark without a lighted lamp, so sometimes, if the girls are nodding, there is a big scramble to get their lamps ready and to get themselves to the place where the ceremony is to take place. Then, once the groom arrives the door is shut, and newcomers are not admitted."

Now, that happened several years ago, but the scene has not changed very much on the west bank of the Jordan from what it was when Jesus was there. Jesus told a similar story about ten bridesmaids. Five had an adequate supply of oil for their lamps and were called wise. There also were five others who did not bring enough oil and had to go out and rouse the oil merchant and purchase some more. While they were doing this, they missed the party.

In my childhood, I used to hear the evangelists tell that story of Jesus in our conservative church, and I always was frightened, because they used the parable as a story of the last judgement. "This is your last chance. Come forward to the mourners' bench and repent. Give up your sinful ways. You may die and not be ready. Repent, repent!"

Even though I had not piled up any great quantity of sins as a child, I was scared! Of course, the evangelists were right in saying that we can turn to God and turn from our sinful ways anytime, and the sooner the better. They were wrong in another way: there is no quick fix in anything.

When I was in junior high school back in Ohio, my mother took me to Cleveland to hear the fiery pianist, Ignace Jan Paderewski. He always packed concert halls wherever he went. In New York, one newspaper headline said of his appearance, "Matinee Girls on Rampage."

Paderewski also had been the Prime Minister of Poland in 1919, and later when his country was overrun by Nazi and Soviet armies, he was the revered elder statesman of the Polish government in exile. Today Paderewski is best known, perhaps, for his famous statement on persistence and discipline, "If I don't practice for one day, I know it. If I don't practice for two days, the critics know it. If I don't practice for three days, the audiences know it." No quick fix.

There are many things you cannot prepare suddenly. In baseball, if the batter is to become a hitter, he needs absolute concentration on the ball as it leaves the pitcher's hand toward him. He must give total attention to determine whether the ball is a curve, a slider, a change of pace, or a fast ball coming toward him at speeds sometimes over 90 miles an hour. The batter must be focused, disciplined.

In fact, NOTHING let loose ever does anything creative. No horse serves a useful purpose until it is harnessed. No energy—gasoline, steam, or nuclear power—ever does anything until it is confined. No scientist thinks he can do as he pleases. Tackle any new problem in the lab, and there are many ways of finding nothing. Only one way leads to the particular truth the scientist seeks.

Think how much extra time football players must put in the weight room—grunting, groaning, and bench pressing weights. Others do extra laps after practice or run up and down the seats of the stadium to build endurance or agility. There are some things you cannot prepare quickly.

Now, really, most of us know that. Much as we complain or rebel or say we would rather be doing anything else than what we are doing, we know that THE EASY LIFE ISN'T ALL IT'S CRACKED UP TO BE.

You see, Jesus is not so much a painter of beautiful ideals as he is a proclaimer of universal laws. Free living is not freedom from the laws of life. Free thinking is not freedom from the laws of thought. Scientific creativity is obedience to scientific law. Artistic creativity is obedience to certain ideals of beauty.

No one is free, until he or she is mastered.

Mark Twain, the great American writer, once fell heavily into debt. According to public law, he could have escaped responsibility in bankruptcy. Why did Mark Twain assume the burden of those debts, even though it meant going around the world as he approached old age, tirelessly speaking and writing, until he had paid the last penny? In one climactic sentence, Mark Twain tells the secret when he says, "Honor is a harder master than the law." There was something inside him that he had to live up to. There are some things you cannot do quickly.

Preachers are often tempted to think of loose living as sin, but loose, undisciplined living is psychological and emotional disintegration. Only a person who has been mastered by something worth being mastered by ever can be much of a person. In fact, there are only two ways to achieve ordered societies: either we must discipline ourselves within or have discipline imposed from without. Little by little, we become what we finally are. A person does not gain 20 pounds overnight. He does it a chocolate bar at a time. A person does not become an alcoholic in one weekend.

On late night TV awhile ago, there was an old James Cagney movie. The scene was a tavern, and Cagney stood at the bar drinking. His wife came in the door of the bar and called, "Jim, come on home." Slowly he turned to her, and just as deliberately, he said, "I am home."

But if a person becomes an alcoholic by so many single drinks, the opposite also is true. We become good people by so many single right thoughts and good deeds.

This is the whole point of the parable of the wise and foolish bridesmaids. When the clock strikes twelve, you cannot begin to do what you should have been doing when it struck six. Neither saints nor prostitutes are made suddenly. You cannot possess a good life by being good once in awhile, anymore than you can possess learning by reading now and then.

In the nineteenth century, the Danish philosopher, Soren Kierkegaard, became the originator of existentialism. He tells about a wild duck who saw some domestic ducks in a barnyard eating grain a farmer had scattered on the ground. Since the wild duck was hungry, he alighted in the barnyard and began to feast. Then the duck found it was comfortable there, and he stayed with the barnyard ducks that day and all through the summer, growing fatter and feeling more comfortable.

When the fall came and the wild ducks flew overhead on their way south, something stirred within him. He flapped his wings and rose as high as the eaves of the barn, but no higher. He had taken on too much weight and had too little exercise.

Then he thought of the comfortable life in the barnyard so down he fluttered and there he stayed. Each spring and fall, as the wild ducks flew overhead, he would look up, flap his wings a bit, and settle back into the old life. Finally he did not even look up.

You see, there is no quick fix, just as there are no crash courses in physical fitness for ducks who want to fly south.

And there is no way to keep your lamp burning when you have squandered your oil and the stores are closed and you are certainly going to miss the party.

###

CHAPTER 22

Naked and Running Away

THE POWER TO STOP RUNNING

Many times I have confessed that I never wanted to be a minister. I never wanted to preach the Christian gospel. I never thought I would enjoy seminary. "All those pious people. I'll go to business school, though, and give lots of money. Okay, Lord?" God was talking to me, and I wanted to run. "No, no, not me. I'm not the type. I do not want to be in the middle of things."

In the Gospel according to Mark there is a story of Jesus, after finishing his last supper with his disciples, going with Peter, James, and John into the Garden of Gethsemane. While the three disciples slept, Jesus prayed in agony, not wanting to face crucifixion.

Immediately after that comes the great drama when Judas, the betrayer, comes with soldiers carrying swords and clubs from the chief priests, scribes, and elders. There is an incident that is seldom mentioned, and Mark tells it this way, "A young man followed . . . with nothing but a linen cloth about his body; and

they seized him, but he left the linen cloth and ran away naked."
The other Gospels do not include that incident. Why not?

Some scholars think that perhaps the young man was Mark himself, and this was Mark's way of saying, "I was there," without mentioning his own name. These same scholars have concluded that the Upper Room where Jesus had eaten his last supper with his disciples might have belonged to the mother of Mark. Mark, still a youth and not yet a disciple, was present in the shadows at the last supper without anyone noticing him.

When Jesus and his disciples left the Upper Room, it was time for a boy like Mark to be in bed. Instead, Mark slipped out of his room with only the linen bed sheet over his naked body. At least that could explain where the narrative about the Garden of Gethsemane came from. If all the disciples were asleep, HOW DID ANYONE KNOW about the spiritual struggle Jesus had in the garden? A young man in the shadows could have seen it.

When Judas and the police arrived to arrest Jesus, Mark himself was very nearly arrested in the scuffle that followed. He could never forget that night, and for those who read his Gospel between the lines, he was saying, "When I was young, I, too, was there."

"A young man followed . . . with nothing but a linen cloth about his body; and they seized him, but he left the linen cloth and ran away naked." He ran, wanting to be in the shadows, but God found him and chose him to tell the story for all history.

For years many people have been saying they love God. All kinds of pious people write articles in Christian magazines or tell on TV how they searched for God all their lives and finally found him. That may be true—there are times when we DO want God. But there also are times WHEN WE RUN from God.

Martin Luther, who more than anyone else began the Protestant Reformation, asked himself truthfully, "How can I say that I love God, when I don't even WANT a God? I want to be my own God!" And so do you. And so did I. I did not want to be a minister. I wanted to be a Christian on my own terms. So I ran. I ran.

Francis Thompson wrote a poem in which he described his own flight from God in *The Hound Of Heaven*:

I fled him down the nights and down the days;
I fled him down the arches of the years;
I fled him down the labyrinthine ways
Of my own mind; and in the midst of tears
I hid from him . . .

No matter what he sought after, he said, it failed to give life any meaning. He was hungry, but he did not know what he was hungry for. He ran from God, ran until God found him and spoke to him:

All things betray thee
Who betrayest me . . .

Isn't it strange how we think we do not want something when we do? A child is tired and worn out, and it is bed time. Mother or father suggests going to bed, "No, I don't wanta!" A teenage boy is teased about liking some girl but would not admit it for anything. And when we grow up, someone asks if we would like to be president of the company where we work, and we say, "No, I wouldn't take that job for anything in the world. Too many headaches." Yet, we jump at it, if the job is offered.

A girl sat in her minister's study, and her minister asked her bluntly, "Tell me, do you feel that ever in your life you have been loved?"

Loved? By whom? My parents? They had to get married because I was coming. They certainly didn't love me. I never seem to fit in. I've never had what I could call real friends. People just don't seem to like me. But do you know something? I DON'T CARE!

All the minister could ask was this, "If you don't care, why are you so heart broken about it?"

You see, the human heart cries for the assurance that someone does care. Without that knowledge, we die. So we stand before God. We stand before God with all the saints, naked and vulnerable, wanting to run. Yet, when we do find love, it has to start with Jesus on the cross, "For God so loved the world . . . ."

The Archbishop of Paris was preaching from the pulpit of Notre Dame Cathedral. He told about three young men who had, years before, been drunk and banged their way into that sanctuary. One of the young men dared another to make a false confession to the priest. He accepted the bet, but the old priest to whom he went saw something much deeper. He said, "My son, you have made your confession, now go into the chapel and look up at the Christ hanging on the cross. Look up into his face and say, 'All this you did for me, and I don't give a damn!'"

The young reveler had been to confession and afterward went back to his friends and tried to collect his bet. The others would not pay, though, until he had done his penance. So he went into the chapel. He stared at the face on the cross and said, "All this you did for me, but I don't . . . ." He could not get any farther.

The archbishop closed his story then by saying, "I was that young man."

And that is where we are. All our cockiness, our self assurance, our indifference, and our don't-give-a-damn attitude has been drained out of us. We have been running, running until God catches us. Then we know that on the cross God was not trying to give us a set of rules, restrictions, or negatives. He was saying, "I'm here in the struggle with you. I love you this much."

###

CHAPTER 23

The Two Kinds of Faith in God

WHY JESUS IS CALLED CHRIST

We all have problems: losing a contract, a friend's terminal illness, getting a new job, getting married, getting unmarried. Sometimes it is just little things, like being late for work or Johnny spilling his milk at breakfast or Mrs. Smith not inviting you to her luncheon, when all your friends are invited. We all have problems, but often they can cause us to avoid the important things in life.

The Russian novelist, Leonid Andreyev, wrote a story entitled *The Day Of The Crucifixion*. It is one of the shortest stories Andreyev ever wrote. Here is the first sentence:

> On that terrible day when the universal injustice was committed, and Jesus Christ was crucified between robbers on Golgotha—on that day from early morning, Ben Tovit, a tradesman of Jerusalem, suffered from . . . a toothache.

The crucifixion then is described as it appears to a person preoccupied with a toothache.

Once in awhile, Ben Tovit becomes aware of the procession of the cross, but soon he goes back to his own private woes. His wife urges him to look at the men on the way to the execution. It would be a diversion.

Here is the author's description of the event:

One of the men, he of the long, light hair in a torn, blood-stained cloak, stumbled over a stone that was thrown under his feet, and he fell. The shouting grew louder, and the crowd, like colored sea water, closed in about the man on the ground. Ben Tovit suddenly shuddered . . . he felt [pain go] through his tooth . . . . He groaned and walked away.

Afterward Ben Tovit was taken by a friend to see "the criminals on the crosses," but did not stay. As Andreyev put it, "He was eager to finish the story of his toothache."

There isn't any need to tack a moral on this story, except to say that most of us are torn by pain, injustices, slights, and annoyances that keep us from coping with life.

Dr. Viktor Frankl is an eminent psychiatrist and author of the world renowned book, *Man's Search For Meaning.* Dr. Frankl is a Jew and was imprisoned by the Nazis in World War II. His wife, his children, and his parents were all killed in the holocaust. When the Gestapo arrested Dr. Frankl, they made him take off all his clothes, and he stood there totally naked. They noticed he still had on his wedding band, but they removed even that from him.

As they were doing this, Frankl said to himself, "You can take away my wife, you can take away my children, and you can strip me of my clothes and my freedom, but there is one thing no person *ever* can take away from me! I STILL CAN CHOOSE HOW I WILL REACT TO WHAT HAPPENS TO ME!"

That was the birth of an idea that many years later Dr. Frankl would develop into his "logotherapy," which is a form of therapy that has helped thousands deal with what life hands them. Many of us face important choices, and we CHOOSE to be miserable. Did you get that? We choose to be miserable. It is a choice. Or we can choose to be happy.

Did you ever stop to think that it is not difficult to have faith in God on our Palm Sundays, when everything seems to be going our way, when the crowds shout approval, and life throws palm branches in our path. Then life goes from Palm Sunday to a garden of decision, when we are about to be crucified. We make a choice how we will react, and the choice determines the kind of person we are.

Dr. E. Stanley Jones was a renowned missionary in India some years ago. He tells how, early in his ministry in India, he tried to escape a serious physical breakdown caused by nervous exhaustion. He tried to escape by running from himself. He tried a furlough in America, and that did not take care of the exhaustion. He tried a rest cure in the cool hills of India. Still no relief.

Then one night in prayer, a Voice unexpectedly seemed to say to him, "Are you really ready for this work I've called you to do?"

Jones said he replied, "No, Lord, I'm done for. I've reached the end of my resources."

The Voice replied, "If you will turn that over to me and not worry about it, I'll take care of it."

Jones thought about it, then said, "Lord, I close the bargain right here." Jones has said about that day, "A great peace settled into my heart . . . . For days after that I hardly knew I had a body. I went through the days, working all day and far into the night, and came to bedtime wondering why in the world I should ever go to bed at all. I seemed possessed by life, and peace, and rest, by Christ himself."

Years later I heard Stanley Jones tell about that incident. He said that many times since then people have asked him whether the experience has faded. He would say, "No, I still work 16 hours a day, and speak on the average of three times a day, but from that day to this, I HAVE NEVER KNOWN A TIRED, EXHAUSTED DAY."

Did you ever think that in the Garden of Gethsemane Jesus might have had another choice than the cross? William Zukerman made that idea into a story entitled *The Refugee From Judea.* He begins with the question, "Suppose Jesus ran for his life on the night of Gethsemane . . . . Suppose that instead of accepting God's will, he had insisted on his own. If that had happened," Zukerman says, "our gospels never could have been written in the form we now have them."

The Garden of Gethsemane story might read this way, "So Jesus took with him Peter and James and John . . . . When they had hidden themselves among the shadows, they soon disappeared out of the garden . . . . During the next day, while the Feast of the Passover was being observed, the three secretly crossed the border . . . and made their way into Egypt."

Then Mr. Zukerman asks, "Wouldn't it have been the sane, practical . . . thing to do?" Mr. Zuckerman spins the fantasy even further. In Egypt, Jesus would have found himself in a much different atmosphere. The people were more tolerant of unconventional ideas. In fact, in Egypt, Jesus might have won a following because of the charm of his personality, his simplicity, and the colorful contrast between his beautiful parables and the dry Greek philosophers. Throngs would have followed him, and in later years, it is possible that Jesus might have returned to Judea and built a spa for himself on the shores of the Dead Sea, in addition to the mansion he owned in Alexandria.

Why didn't it happen that way?

In many ways, the idea is attractive. A lot of us would have used that way out. We could have escaped death, and possibly have become famous and wealthy with a big TV show.

BUT JESUS COULD NOT HAVE BEEN CALLED CHRIST IF HE HAD MADE THAT CHOICE. In a few short years, the world would have forgotten him, even forsaken him for other, more popular preachers.

You see, there really are two kinds of faith in God. As Harry Emerson Fosdick writes, "One says IF . . . if all goes well, if life is hopeful, prosperous, happy, THEN I will believe in God. The other says THOUGH . . . though the forces of evil triumph, though everything goes wrong and Gethsemane comes and the cross looms, I still choose to follow."

The Bible is full of this contrast. On the one hand, Jacob is saying, "If God will be with me, and will give me bread to eat, and clothes to put on, so that I come again to my father's house, THEN the Lord shall be my God." Fosdick continues by saying that is "fair weather faith": we will trust God if everything is okay, but in Gethsemane, that kind of faith collapses.

Listen to the other kind of faith, he says, beginning not with IF, but with THOUGH. "Though he kill me, yet will I trust in him . . . . Though I walk through the valley of the shadow of death, I will fear no evil, for you, God are with me . . . Though the waters roar and be troubled, though the mountains shake . . . the Lord of hosts is with us . . . ."

So it is not on Palm Sunday with its hosannas but in Gethsemane that the real choice comes. And THE CHOICES WE MAKE DECIDE THE KIND OF PERSON WE ARE. In a sense, Palm Sunday represents success, and Gethsemane represents failure. On Palm Sunday, hosannas fill the air and palm branches line the road, but in Gethsemane our hopes are dashed, our prayers are denied, and . . . we . . . sweat blood. Yet, out of the world's Gethsemanes have come the people we find it impossible to forget.

In the Explorers Club of New York City, there are a number of notable exhibits: photographs from Admiral Richard Byrd's flights over the North and South Poles, artifacts from Lowell

Thomas' early explorations into the Himalayan Mountains, and pieces of the moon brought back by the first expedition there.

What has captured my attention the most was an old sledge used by Roald Amundsen and the journal of Captain Robert Scott in their great race of 1911 and 1912 to be the first person to discover the South Pole. Captain Scott made it on January 17, 1912, only to find that the Norwegian explorer, Amundsen, had beaten him.

In fact, Scott did not even come back. Sickness, insufficient food, and severity of the weather made traveling extremely slow on the sledges of that day, until at last a blizzard prevented all possibilities of going on. The party perished on or about March 27. Eight months later, searchers found Scott's tent, the bodies of the little group, and the journals kept by Scott.

So Scott did not come back. His prayer was not answered. He failed. But there are a few sentences the world will never forget. He wrote, "I do not regret this journey . . . . We took risks . . . we knew that we took them. Things have come out against us, and therefore we have no cause for complaint, but bow to the will of Providence still to do our best to the last . . . ."

Here is one of the mysteries of life: the amazing success of failure. In a sense, as the world saw it, Jesus too was a failure. Every year when Lent comes, we are confronted by the fact that we are celebrating a failure. Here is a person whose nation rejected him, whose family did not understand him, and whose government crucified him. Even on Calvary he cried, "My God, my God, why have *you* forsaken me?"

How strange to think that nearly 2,000 years afterward, with awe and adoration we bow to worship so great a failure.

###

CHAPTER 24

The Foolishness of the Cross

THE ABSURD REASONABLENESS OF GOD

The musical play *Godspell* is about the life of Christ, and the disciples are all dressed as clowns. Jesus himself is in whiteface and wears a T-shirt with a large Superman "S" on the front. I have seen the musical twice, but I will never forget my initial reaction. It was almost disbelief, or at least dismay, that Jesus should be presented in this way. As the musical unfolded, though, I began to see what the writers and producers were getting at.

All of us are foolish, aren't we? At least a little bit? And I remembered the words of Paul written to the church in Corinth, "What seems to be God's foolishness is wiser than our wisdom, and what seems to be God's weakness is stronger than our strength." At the end of the musical, I was unusually moved when they carried Jesus, still in whiteface, off to be crucified.

At the final curtain, the audience was invited to come to the stage and have wine out of gallon jugs with members of the cast. It did, indeed, seem to me like a sacrament.

Several years after the death and resurrection of Jesus, Paul wrote to the little church in the corrupt, party city of Corinth,

"The message of the cross is foolishness to those on the way to ruin, but to us who are on the way to salvation, it is the power of God."

To many Corinthians, the cross WAS foolishness. Corinth was in ancient Greece, the second city in the nation and only 45 miles from Athens. Here were hills dotted with marble temples and shrines filled with scores of gods and goddesses. In Corinth, there was extreme wealth and luxury, and you could hear philosophers discoursing about the enjoyment of life.

In Jerusalem, there had been an ugly rock outside the city where Jesus of Nazareth was crucified as a criminal. Foolishness?

Paul continued, "It is written, 'I will destroy the wisdom of the wise, and frustrate the cleverness of the clever.'" Later he said, "The Jews demand miracles and Greeks seek wisdom, but we preach Christ crucified . . . ."

In 54 A.D., shortly after the time of Jesus, a man from Egypt arrived in Jerusalem claiming to be the Messiah. He persuaded 20,000 people to follow him to the Mount of Olives by promising that at his command the walls of Jerusalem would fall down. That was the kind of thing the Jews were looking for! In Jesus, they saw one who deliberately avoided the spectacular.

"And the Greeks seek wisdom." It is true. The Greeks earlier had been seekers of wisdom, but that search had degenerated into an intoxication with fine words, kind of a mental gymnastics with no real interest in solutions. Paul, a Christian with his strange message about the cross, appeared to have little chance of being heard. Yet, today we hear again Paul's words, "What seems to be God's foolishness is wiser than our wisdom, and what seems to be God's weakness is stronger than our strength."

In New York City, there was a group of Quakers who heard there was to be an ugly confrontation between young protesters and some hardhats. The Quakers went as a group and positioned themselves between the two factions as they converged, absorbing the hostility and punishment of both protesters and hardhats, until finally the combatants began to see what was happening. Then quietly, and somewhat sadly, both sides withdrew, touched deeply by those Quakers who were fools for Christ's sake.

In his diary, Soren Kierkegaard told about a service of worship held in the palace for the king and queen and their court. This, of course, was a select circle of affluent and distinguished people. The court chaplain preached a moving sermon on the words of the Apostle Paul, "God chose the lowly and despised." Kierkegaard commented, "Nobody laughed."

The fool. The holy fool.

I think of Charlie Brown and Linus in the comic strip *Peanuts* standing together pondering the meaning of life. The first to speak is Charlie Brown, "I think I can understand your fear of libraries, Linus . . . . You fear the library rooms because they are strange to you . . . . You are out of place . . . . All of us have certain areas in which we feel out of place."

"In for On YOU feel out of place, Charlie Brown?"

"Earth."

Maybe Charlie Brown has something, something every Christian knows, however dimly, that we are all a little uncomfortable in this world, where success sometimes means compromising principles and ideals. Here the blessings of jet planes can be turned into fighters, and the peaceful advantages of nuclear power can be made into bombs. Here the computer can be used for hate as well as love, and survival of the fittest often means survival of the LEAST human.

So Paul concluded this passage from I Corinthians 1:18-27, "God chose what is foolish to shame the wise, and God chose what is weak to shame the strong." Wasn't that the cross? Weakness? God is saying, "I love you so much I sent my son, my only son. I am in the struggle with you." And here we are, over 2,000 years later, talking about the power of that love.

God's love IS power. For instance, we have known for a long time that many who seek medical aid really are suffering from fear, worry, and anger. One of the Mayo brothers estimated that 60% of all the patients who come to the Mayo Clinic would not need to come, if their lives were in tune with God and people.

There is an old Hassidic story that says everyone must have two pockets into which he can reach from time to time as need requires. In the one pocket is written, "I am but dust and ashes." In the other pocket, "For my sake were the heavens and earth created."

A young man was in a social studies class in college, and he had been asked to draw a line down the center of the page. At the top of the left column, he wrote LIABILITIES, and at the top of the right column, he wrote ASSETS. Then, shielding the page from the girl across the aisle, under LIABILITIES he printed:

Impatient
Demanding
Proud
Moody
Filled with doubt

Then he began to contemplate the ASSETS column. With another look to be sure the girl could not see the page, he printed:

A child of God

You see, for all our liabilities, confusion, and the ordinariness of our lives, we have been chosen by a God who, for some strange reason, delights in us. In Psalm 107, the Psalmist writes, "O give thanks to the Lord, for he is good, and his love endures forever! Let the redeemed of the Lord say so!"

Now, that is a shattering statement. God loves us! God delights in us. And, as the psalmist continues, God does all kinds of absurd things, such as turning a desert into pools of water and satisfying the thirsty, and filling the hungry with good things, and bringing people out of gloom and delivering them from their distresses. Then we, too, do absurd things, such as:

> taking care of people who are not our own,
> sending needy black teenagers off to colleges,
> teaching simple methods of agriculture so the poor of the earth can feed themselves,
> turning the desert into pools of water through our knowledge of irrigation,
> and building sound and inexpensive housing in undeveloped nations.

Surprisingly, then, we ask the benevolence committee in our church to think up more projects, so we can give more money, and be unselfish . . . and foolish for Christ's sake.

In Herb Gardner's play, *A Thousand Clowns*, Murray does not act pious, but I think he speaks deeply about the things of God. He has been a pretty unconventional guardian for his young nephew, so a social worker comes to see about taking the boy away. Murray talks about the child's future and also about our vocations as holy fools. He says:

> I just want him to stay with me 'til I can be sure he won't turn into Norman Nothing, one of the nice, dead people. I want him to get to know exactly the special thing he is. I want him to stay awake and know who the phonies are. I want him to know how to holler and put up an argument before I let him go.

I want to be sure he sees all the wild possibilities. I want him to know the subtle, important reason why he was born a human being, and not a chair.

Doesn't that say it all—that God's foolishness is God's absurd reasonableness, and his weakness is stronger than our strength?

Surprising as it may sound, Rabbi Abraham Heschel has written,

> God has so ordered this world
> that every little girl may be a princess
> and every little boy a prince.

And somehow you and I, despite any evidence to the contrary, will continue to believe that we are not just people who perform tasks but ones who weep and laugh and hope and pray in an . . . incredible . . . world. That we are made for eternity, and what is more, WE ARE GOING TO MAKE IT TO ETERNITY!

> O give thanks to the Lord for he is good.
> HIS LOVE ENDURES FOREVER.
> Let the redeemed of the Lord say so!
> HIS LOVE ENDURES FOREVER!

###

CHAPTER 25

Living with Perpetual Emergency

CHRISTIANITY IS A REVOLUTION!

Today we are living in a "state of perpetual emergency," as someone called it, and I do not suppose anyone would dispute that. We have seen the dissolution of the Soviet Union. There was armed conflict in the Balkans. We fought a war called Desert Storm, then another war in the same area called Iraqi Freedom.

Before that there was Tienenman Square and Vietnam and the Korean War, which started just five years after World War II, and, of course, World War I, "The War to End All Wars." We are living in the middle of a revolution, and it does not startle anyone when I write that, because we are used to it.

In fact, we have been living in a time of tumult or technological upheaval for years. In the memory of many, we have progressed from squawky party telephones to direct dial calls to London or Honolulu or Ranchipoor. Some who were bumping along in jerky gasoline engines only a few years ago now are sitting in airports waiting for jets. Those who once were entertained by a family picture album now doze in front of a color TV and choose among a football or baseball game or a dozen movies in a single weekend. And there are fax machines and e-mail, not just special delivery letters, and genetic engineering and modems and micro chips and the Internet.

Christianity itself was born in a revolution, or to be more accurate, Christianity IS a revolution. In the days of Jesus, the city of Rome was emptied of fashionable people, because they wanted to escape the heat, smells, and urban congestion, as well as the threat of typhoid and malaria. The upper class Romans would flee 100 miles southeast to the rocky, sunny shores of the Bay of Naples and the part of the area now called Sorrento.

Pagan Holiday, by Tony Perrottet, tells that on warm summer nights the hills echoed with the sounds of nude swimming parties and drunken carousing. Later, in the time of the emperors Tiberius, Caligula, and Nero, as the Christian church was beginning, the Bay of Naples became a place where Romans "indulged in prodigious bouts of eating, drinking and fornication . . . [and] noblewomen went incognito as prostitutes."

What sort of world would this be today if the Roman Empire could have endured? It was a great, sprawling, corrupt system, as merciless as it was mighty, built on the tired backs of slaves.

Later, as the New Testament book of Hebrews was being written, persecution of the Christians was a "perpetual emergency." In the 12th chapter of Hebrews, it says, "Yet once more I will shake not only the earth, but also the heavens . . . in order that what cannot be shaken may remain." This is not merely a text of scripture. It is a philosophy, an interpretation of history. God, says the ancient preacher, periodically shakes the world.

We do not know very much about the writer of those words. In fact, there has been a debate lasting for over a thousand years about who was the author of the Book of Hebrews. It has been suggested that this letter was not a letter at all but a sermon preached by a living minister to a living congregation, a "live show."

Visualize, if you will, an eloquent, Godly man with long robes standing in some hidden cave with his back to the wall of rock. He is looking in the faces of a small group of his Jewish friends, people who had dared death and persecution to be part of the sect called Christians.

Many historians say without hesitation that this period, the time from the fire of Rome under Nero to the fall of Jerusalem under Titus, was the most beastly and brutal era through which humanity ever passed. It was a time of revolution, 70 A.D. Jewish Christians looked at their ruined city: the temple, the sacrifice, the priesthood — everything they had been taught to believe was permanent — was gone.

I suppose what panics people the most in a revolutionary time is that they think everything will be lost if the world is upset. That is not necessarily the case. During the Protestant Reformation in the 16th century, Martin Luther said, "Here I stand, God help me, I can do no other." God was shaking the world. The issues that thundered around his German head were the protests of a people against an evil that had become intolerable. They were afraid that if the Roman Catholic mass were taken away, religion itself would not survive. But it did.

In the 19th century, when Edmund Burke was alive, he complained, "The age of chivalry has gone." To that we would say, "Thank God!" Who wants plumed knights with steel armor riding in jet planes or on a moped?

Margaret Mitchell wrote a book about the plantation and mint julep days of the American Confederacy. Then she said wistfully, "Gone . . . gone with the wind." There are many who thank the Lord, for those were days of slavery for some and poverty for many.

Some years ago, there was a night of terror in a small Alabama town where blacks lived. An unusually brilliant shower of meteors criss-crossed the heavens and threw fear into the hearts of the blacks. They were uneducated folk and knew nothing of asteroids and meteors. All they knew was that the stars were falling and "judgement day was comin'."

Up on the hill, though, there was an old school teacher who lived in a cabin, and some of them ran up to the old man to ask what to do. They found him sitting on the door step of his cabin, looking up and enjoying the great show. They were shocked that he could be so calm. "Look at' em now," he said, "ain't they purty? Look at them little bitty stars shootin' cross the sky."

"But Mose, ain't you feared?"

"Course I ain't feared. Look yonder at them big stars; they's still a-shinin'. Go to bed, chillun, them big stars ain't moved an inch."

Today we may be in the middle of one of the great upheavals of history. The idea of colonialism, whether by Britain, Russia, or the United States has been shaken. The idea that white, Anglo-Saxon males are supreme has been shaken. The basic idea of materialism, that people CAN live by bread and machines, is being shaken. The idea that a person is self-sufficient is being shaken. It may be that the first century preacher is saying to our day, "Yet once more, says the Lord, I shake the earth . . .."

I suppose it is comforting to think that everybody wants the best and will automatically work things out, if you just give them time. But that is only half true. The other half is that people also are mentally and morally lazy, and sometimes we do not want to be disturbed, even for the better.

Even so, not everything that is happening is wrong. God shakes us to stir up progress. There are people awakening today to the fact that faith makes a difference. They are getting into prayer and service and worship and stewardship. They are beginning to discover the Word of God and what it can mean in our day.

On a Monday after Easter, there was a picture published in the *New York Times* among other pictures of Easter festivities. It was so startling because of its contrast with the bright Easter outfits on the sidewalks farther down Fifth Avenue, and it caused comment all over the nation. It was the picture of a young black man dressed in blue jeans and a T-shirt, hanging on a cross in a vacant lot among the run down tenements of East Harlem.

Someone went to investigate, and they found the answer in the East Harlem Protestant Parish. The parish is in the indescribably run-down tenement and slum area from about 96th to 110th streets and from Fifth Avenue to the East River. There are many blacks, Italians, and Puerto Ricans living there; and because of the explosive environment, gang wars are frequent.

The East Harlem Protestant Parish works with alcoholics, drug addicts, the homeless, and juvenile delinquents. One of their deaconesses was a former Communist organizer.

On Good Friday that year, they decided to re-enact on the streets and lots of East Harlem the story of the original Good Friday. Instead of using Biblical robes, they dressed in jeans and T-shirts. The young man chosen to portray Christ was black. The disciples were Italians, blacks, and Puerto Ricans.

The Good Friday procession started from one of the store-front churches, and the black acting the part of Jesus began to carry his cross through the streets of Harlem. Strangely enough, no one laughed. Some began to follow. Soon there was a crowd, just as there had been on that first Good Friday.

Finally, the procession reached the vacant lot where the crucifixion was to take place. The lot was filled with rubble, and around it were the poorest types of tenements. Some of those living in the tenements became curious and leaned out of their windows to see what was happening.

Later they joined the mob below in making a noisy tumult. When Pontius Pilate said, "Shall I crucify your king?" they all shouted, "Crucify him, crucify him, crucify him!" Then they roped Jesus to his cross.

After awhile, Christ bowed his head and spoke quietly, but the crowd was so hushed, everyone could hear him, "Father, forgive them, for they know not what they do." The people understood this, because he was talking to their need.

Christianity today still is a revolution. It is a revolt against poverty, against homelessness, against violence, against the religious ignorance of our children, against sensuality, against despair. No longer are ministers simply street corner evangelists. We need ministers for the up and out, as well as the down and out. We need counselors in urban parishes and ranchers in the churches of the western mountains.

We also need doctors and nurses and teachers and social workers and administrators and athletes and students and farmers—Christians who are convinced that God can speak to the people of our day.

###

CHAPTER 26

The Risk Factor in Faith

THERE IS RISK EVEN IN A CRUCIFIXION

Ultimately, everything in life depends on faith—not necessarily what we call religious faith but faith nevertheless. Ultimately, everything in life depends on faith.

There were two men climbing a mountain that never before had been climbed. They were high above a precipice and were roped together headed for the top. Suddenly, the foot of one of them slipped. He lost his balance and fell, jerking his companion from his feet. They began to slide with increasing speed down the icy slope—faster and faster toward the precipice.

Let me interrupt this story for a moment to remind you that this is a chapter about risk, about gambling, which really is what faith is all about.

Back to the story: as the two men continue sliding down the mountainside, let's remind ourselves of what they started out to do. When people climb mountains, they are roped together for two reasons. They help each other in danger, and they increase their efficiency in reaching the top. They do not make any signed promises, but all climbers know the tradition of the mountains: the two people are one. They belong to each other.

These two men had climbed step by step up the mountain and were watched by friends in the base camp below. Suddenly, in the field of the telescope, the tragic slip is seen. The watchers are terrified but helpless. There is a moment of hope, as the speed of the slide decreases, because of the desperate efforts of the two climbers to brake their fall. In spite of all they can do, though, the rear man reaches the edge of the precipice and goes over. The upper man still is on the slope, digging frantically to stop his slide. The rear man hangs helpless, dangling in the air.

Then horror strikes the watchers again, as they see a new tragedy. The rope suddenly seems to snap, breaking at the very edge of the precipice. The dangling man falls like a rag doll, bouncing and limp, to his death on the rocks below. As soon as they can, the members of the rescue squad climb to the exhausted survivor. They look about, see the frayed end of the rope and beside it a knife. The rope had not broken; the survivor had cut it.

The question is this: Was it right for the man to cut the rope? Make the question as hard as you can. Say he could not have saved the man below and would have died himself, if he had not cut the rope. Say the climber was married and had a family to support. Say he was a brilliant scientist with a great experiment unfinished.

Remember in answering the question, however, that he was married and he was a scientist BEFORE he took the risk and tied up with his fellow climber. Was it right for him to cut the rope?

Simon Peter once cut the rope. He was tied to a young Galilean, and the young Galilean faced a cross. They were at the house of Caiaphas, the high priest, warming themselves at the fire, waiting for Jesus who was being tried inside. A man nudged the person standing next to him and said, "That looks like one of them." Peter stood on one foot, then on the other, and backed away from the fire, where he could not be seen so well. He backed into a teenage girl who said, "Why, this man was with him!" And Peter swore that he had not been with Jesus.

I suppose Peter was not much worse than any of the other disciples. They had faded away, all of them. They all gambled that death was the end of this business of the Messiah. So the scripture writer explained, "And they brought Jesus to the place Golgotha, which is the Place of the Skull. It was the third hour, and they crucified him. And the soldiers gambled for his garments" (John 19:23-24).

Why not gamble for Christ's seamless robe? He would never need it again. To all the people around the cross, there was nothing so sure as a Roman crucifixion. How wrong they were. There is risk, even in a crucifixion.

Now, at the beginning of this chapter, I said that ultimately, everything in life depends on faith, or risk. In other words, all of life is a gamble. Leaving your home in the morning is a risk. You might slip on the sidewalk. Going up the elevator to your office is a risk. You could stumble. Buying eggs is a risk; buying fish is a risk. In fact, all of business lives on risk, which is to say it lives on credit.

Even such an exact matter as mathematics depends on faith. Yes, it does! Of course, $2 + 2 = 4$ is a fact, and $3 \times 3 = 9$ is a fact. But when you get into higher mathematics, or the philosophy of math, the kind that enabled Einstein to figure that $E = MC_2$, even such a solid subject as mathematics is a belief, or a theory.

There is a great deal of nonsense today about science dealing only with what can be proved. EVERY scientific theory is a leap of faith. We speak of the THEORY of relativity, not the FACT of relativity, but on the basis of the THEORY of relativity, people split the atom.

There is risk in having a family. One little boy lived for several years in his family as an only child. He wanted some brothers and sisters, but for some reason none ever came along. Finally, his mother suggested that, instead of just wishing for brothers and sisters, he should pray for some. So, for several months, every night as he went to bed he prayed that God would grant his request. Nothing happened, so the boy stopped praying.

Then one great day his mother was taken to the hospital and came home after a few days bringing, not just one, not just two, but three brothers and sisters. As the boy examined them with great interest, his father said, "Aren't you glad you prayed?"

And the little boy replied, "Aren't you glad I stopped?" You see, there is risk in prayer, there is risk in having a family, and there is risk in life itself. Like it or not, we MUST live by faith, which is what risk is.

This is precisely the message of Easter: the great heroes of the Bible were called people of faith. They were not always perfect. Occasionally, some were guilty of sin. They were NOT the safe, respectable persons who value comfort or security above everything else. They were people of faith, gamblers for high stakes: justice, mercy, and righteousness. They would hazard their lives for God's sake, and the greatest was the Galilean who dared believe his death could change the world!

You know, sometimes when I think of a group of young people in a church, I am afraid. But my greatest fear is not that they will commit some petty act that displeases the blue-noses in the congregation. My greatest fear for young people is that somehow they will miss life, a sacrificial life, that they will never risk losing their hearts for love, risk going without food for an education, or risk losing their lives to find them.

Jesus himself gambled! He bowed his head and died in confidence that THIS IS GOD'S WORLD. Jesus put down his life on the proposition that God has written truth and righteousness into the very structure of things.

Columbus risked his life on the belief that the world is round. He had no certainty. He staked his life and sailed west. Moses,

Martin Luther, George Washington, Susan B. Anthony, and Martin Luther King bet their lives on the belief that people are entitled to liberty. They had no certainties; they were not even sure they could win. They had nothing but a dream of something that never had existed on earth before. They gambled. They bet their lives on a great dream.

Abraham Lincoln was a risk taker. He ran for the legislature of the state of Illinois and was defeated. He failed in business and worked 17 years to pay the debts of a worthless partner. He was engaged to a lovely girl, but she died. He sought the nomination as his party's candidate for the United States House of Representatives but did not make it. He ran for the U.S. Senate and was defeated by Douglas. Yet, Abraham Lincoln was one of the greatest men America has produced.

After he was killed, his body passed through the city of Albany, New York, where a black woman stood on the curb and lifted her little son as far as she could reach above the heads of the crowd. She said to her son, "Take a long look, honey, he died for you."

I wish I could lift up your hearts to see Calvary. Take a long look. He died for you.

Sometimes in our cynicism, we are tempted to think the loudest forces in the world are also the strongest. See Jesus on the cross, we say. It is like a song bird had been caught and was murdered there. Oh, well, that is life.

But 2,000 years afterward, as someone has said, the song bird is still singing.

In John Masefield's play, *The Trial Of Jesus*, Pilate's wife and the centurion are talking together after the crucifixion. Pilate's wife says, "Do you think he's dead?"

Longinus, the centurion, answers, "No, lady, I don't."

"Then where is he?"

"Let loose in the world, lady, where neither Roman nor Jew can stop his truth."

At the cross, the claps of thunder and the flashes of lightning have stopped. The two figures on the outer crosses are almost still, and the crowd is dwindling on Golgotha, the Hill of the Skull. The figure on the center cross cries out, "Father, into thy hands I commend my spirit," and he dies.

Studdert Kennedy put it into blunt verse when he describes that scene this way;

> And sitting down they watched Him there,
> The soldiers did;
> There, while they played with dice,
> He made his sacrifice,
> And died upon the cross to rid
> God's world of sin.
>
> He was a gambler, too, my Christ.
> He took his life and threw it
> For a world redeemed.

So life always is a gamble. Do we risk anything, anything at all, to be followers of Christ?

###

CHAPTER 27

Getting It All!

THE POWER OF JESUS TODAY

The first word Jesus spoke to his disciples, when he was with them on the evening of his resurrection, was the Hebrew word, "Shalom." The word often is translated peace, but it is more than that. Shalom is joy, abundance, good health, neighborliness, and peace. It is everything God wants us to be physically, mentally, spiritually, and emotionally. It means "Have it all!"

Years ago, Dr. Wilfred Grenfell wanted to improve the health of the people of Labrador. After spending years as a missionary doctor in that cold, northern country, he returned to the United States. He spoke one night about the joy of service. He said that the greatest joy in life is in creativeness, in working with God to make things become finer.

Then Grenfell told about the increasing number of people who are fed up, mostly because they have never found anything outside themselves to fasten to. He said they are a lot like the little barnacles at the seashore. When they are born, they give promise of being free swimming animals. Very early they learn to attach themselves to boat bottoms or the pilings on docks. They grow a hard shell on the outside and spend the rest of their lives hanging on and kicking food into their mouths with their hind legs.

Jesus had a plan for us, a master plan. In the Greek, he called it "metanoia," which means a change in our way of thinking. The great challenge is to give up the old vision and accept the new one. I suspect the disciples had their own ideas of what would make them happy: a boat full of fish, a full stomach, and enough money for a better home for the family. All they thought they needed was a little luck, a calm sea, and a couple good seasons, and they would have it made.

Then along came Jesus who shattered their hopes and self-centered dreams. What they really needed, and what they were slow to accept, was God's plan, metanoia. Jesus had been able to get them away from their boats and nets and little businesses, but they still had their own formulas for happiness. They had their own set of beatitudes, which did not include loving their enemies, giving away their possessions, walking second miles, and turning the other cheek when someone slapped them.

There was a young man who was born seriously myopic. He could see clearly only those objects within a few feet of his eyes. His parents did not think he needed glasses, so he grew up not being able to see clearly, not being able to identify the leaves on trees, and not being able to catch a fly ball in the outfield, because he could not see it until it hit him.

Then one day, when he was eighteen, the boy consulted an eye doctor, and they began experimenting with corrective lenses, until he had the proper prescription. He asked the boy to look out the window. "Wow!" the boy exclaimed, "so beautiful!" For the first time, he could see blue skies and the smiling faces of people and billboards and street signs.

Later he told his minister, "It was the second most beautiful experience of my life." Naturally the minister had to ask what the most beautiful experience was. The boy said, "The day I started taking Jesus seriously, when I felt the warmth of God's love, and saw others as my brothers and sisters in God. That was the beginning of a new life for me."

Metanoia, a change of attitude, a radical change of outlook. This is scary, because change always is. Let's look back to the story of Dr. Wilfred Grenfell, the missionary doctor who spent many years working with the people of that cold, northern country of Labrador. After the service at which he was speaking, a woman came up to Dr. Grenfell and praised him for the great sacrifice he had made in spending his life in Labrador. He said, "Lady, you completely misunderstood me. I was having the time of my life. I never made a sacrifice."

There is a young minister who preached in a large church and said, "There are three points to my sermon." Most people yawned, because they had heard that many times before. The young man went on, "My first point is this: at this time, there are approximately two billion people starving to death in the world." The reaction through the congregation was about the same. They had heard that sort of statement many times before. Then he said, "My second point . . ." Everyone sat up, because he was only ten or fifteen seconds into his sermon and was already on his second point. The young man paused and then said,

"My second point is that most of you don't give a damn."

He paused again, as gasps and rumblings flowed across the congregation, and then said, "My third point is that the real tragedy among Christians today is that many of you are more concerned that I said, 'damn,' than that I said two billion people are starving to death." Then the minister sat down. The whole sermon took less than a minute, but in many ways, it was one of the most powerful sermons ever preached.

The young minister reminded us that we are Christians—not to be perfect, not just to be nice, not even to feel good necessarily, but to get our act together and DO SOMETHING . . . for Christ's dear sake.

I once had a wedding where we came to the question that the minister traditionally asks the father of the bride, "Who gives Shari to be married to Bob?" The usual response would be, "Her mother and I do," or simply, "I do." So, in the accepted manner, the father of the bride said, "I do." Then from the first pew, his wife also piped up, "I do." And Shari's brother, who was in the wedding party, said, "I do." And Shari's sister, also in the wedding ceremony, said, "I do." The whole family was giving Shari away, and by that time, everyone in the sanctuary was laughing.

In a way, though, that is a parable of our world. Today we are all related. We live so closely together we catch each other's diseases. The economy of the Pacific Rim or Europe affect us. So when we ask, "Who gives this person?" someone in Iowa says, "I do," and someone in Japan says, "I do," and someone in Africa says, "I do. I do."

Let's go back to the word "shalom," which means "getting it all." Shalom: nature, animals, and human beings all moving in freedom and peace together. Today many who are older sought for shalom in the suburbs: two chickens in every pot, a car (or two or three cars) in every garage, green grass utterly without a blade of crab grass, and children playing peacefully together, grateful to us, the provider of all this bounty. IT DID NOT WORK OUT THAT WAY!

The kids got bored with Utopia. They went off to find their own shalom and looked for it in communes, in drugs, and in easy sex. They did not find it there, either. They did discover there is syphilis in sex, that loving members of the commune would shirk their share of the work, and there are mosquitoes in paradise. Both elders and kids were seeking personal shalom for US, but that did not bring the peaceable kingdom.

The lesson to be learned is that PEOPLE CANNOT BE PEACEFUL AND LOVING AND HAPPY WHILE OTHERS SUFFER. We are just not made that way. Our shalom is interdependent with others. As the great pioneer Swiss psychiatrist Carl Jung said, "The only way to mental health is in self-giving."

Mabel Shaw was a missionary in Africa. She told her little Bantu children about giving a cup of water to drink in the name of The Chief. The Chief was the name they had learned to call Jesus. "Whoever does this for one of my poorest brothers or sisters," The Chief says, "you do it for me." The boys and girls were tremendously interested, since in that hot, dry country, a cup of cold water can be beyond price.

Not long afterward, Mabel Shaw was watching a string of porters, or burden bearers, come up the village street. They obviously were exhausted, and they sank wearily to rest at the side of the road. Now, these men were from another tribe—that could be seen from their clothes and the way they wore their hair. In Africa, even today, there is suspicion and even hostility between tribes.

Then a surprising thing happened. Out of one of the huts came a small line of children of primary age. Each of them carried a water pot. The children were a little frightened, but they were determined to see it through. They went to the tired bearers, knelt before them, and held out their water pots. "We are The Chief's children," they said, "and we offer you a drink." The astonished bearers knelt in return and took the water and drank. The primary children then took to their heels and ran back to Mabel Shaw.

In an ordinary village, if these burden bearers had asked for a drink, they would have been told, "You are not of our village. Get water yourselves." But in THIS village, the boys and girls said, "We give thirsty people a drink in the name of The Chief."

And The Chief says, "Seek first the kingdom of God and his righteousness, and all these things will be added."

###

CHAPTER 28

Finding Jesus as Lord

POWER TO BECOME

There is a lot of talk today that all religions are pretty much alike, and there is an effort to find something upon which all the great faiths agree. They say that the one thing we all hold in common is our belief in God. We all believe in God, don't we?

In fact, there was a conference recently sponsored by the Presbyterian Church USA, and the Reverend Dirk Ficca, who is director of the Council for the Parliament of the World's Religions, asked the question, "What's the big deal about Jesus?" He suggested that the more emphasis Christians place on Jesus, the greater difficulty we are going to have relating to people of other faiths. He said that God has been working in all times, in all places, and in all religions, not only through Jesus. Certainly Jesus was a great prophet, but not the unique son of God.

As would be expected, these views expressed by Mr. Ficca at a Presbyterian conference caused an explosive reaction in the church.

The remarks of Mr. Ficca were related by Dr. John H. Stevens, senior minister of the 5,000-member First Presbyterian Church of Colorado Springs, Colorado. He said that since Mr. Ficca's statement, almost a thousand congregations have united in a "Confessing Church Movement," which says, "We believe that Jesus Christ is the only Lord of all, and that it is through him we have salvation, according to the Scripture."

Awhile ago, on *The Larry King Show*, there was a panel of religious leaders discussing the common elements in all faiths. Present were the head of the Islamic Association in the United States, two Jewish rabbis, and a couple Christian ministers. During the discussion, it was clear that Larry King, the rabbis, and the Islamic leader wanted to talk about the things that unite us and not those that divide us. We should talk about God, they said, and not about Jesus, because Jesus is divisive.

One of the Christian ministers, a member of the panel, disagreed. He said, "Well, I cannot really talk about God apart from Jesus, because everything that I know about God that's of any significance or importance, I know because of Jesus Christ."

You see, it is not necessarily true that minimizing the beliefs of the different religions of the world will bring harmony and peace. For instance, in 1844, Mirza Ali Muhammad tried to take what he thought to be the best of each faith and combine them in a new religion called Bahai.

He taught the oneness of the human race, the equality of the sexes, and the need for equality of opportunity to freely search for truth. He said that true worship is work that improves the harmony or happiness of the human race. He wrote more than 100 books expounding his teachings and called on the leaders of the nations to form a world government.

Muslim fundamentalists disagreed with his teachings and violently persecuted the Bahai'ists. Thousands were killed, their homes destroyed, and their places of worship burned or torn down. Even their cemeteries were desecrated.

In the interest of accuracy, it is also not true that all religions believe in God. Buddha did not believe in a preeminent, transcendent, but also personal God, and neither did Confucius. In fact, there are many basic differences among religions. For instance, we all have powerful impulses or drives in us, and these are the forces that make our lives. What we should do with these impulses is the basis for all religions, all philosophies, and all great systems of ethics and government.

One answer would be to let these impulses run wild, since these forces are natural. What is natural should be right, and according to this philosophy, wrong would be suppressing our natural passions.

During World War II, Hitler and the Nazis took this philosophy, as expounded by Frederick Nietzsche, and put it into government. Nietzsche said, "You have heard how it was said in old times, 'Blessed are the meek, for they shall inherit the earth.' But I say to you, 'Blessed are the valiant, for they shall make the earth their throne. Get rid of your pious priests and their weak-livered gospel of mercy . . .. Be strong, be a superman.'"

That leads directly to another answer, which is the extreme opposite of total freedom. This answer says that our primitive desires, our driving forces, are so fierce that we must find a way to reduce them. Buddhism and Hinduism are the great religions dedicated to the elimination of desire. Buddha saw desire as the source of all evil and conflict. He said, "You must free your soul of desire . . .. Denude your heart of every want, and in utterly passionless existence you will find peace of mind, contentment, and after much practice come at last to Nirvana, the state of nothingness."

There is a third answer to what should be done with the great driving forces of our lives. It is not to let our impulses run wild. It is not to eliminate desire. It is the answer of Christ, where we find fulfillment. In Jesus, we encounter power to:

Turn on your life

Be meek
    Pray when you do not know how
        Use your tiredness
            Prevail

Win by losing
    Be significant
        Love the unlovable
            Be genuine
                Change

Resist
    Find peace
        Find joy
            Stop running
                Become children of God

I.   FINDING JESUS AS LORD

The first great statement of faith, or creed, of the Christian church was "Jesus Is Lord." In the Old Testament, the rabbis used the words *Yahway* or *Adonai* to refer to Lord or God. Both words meant Lord God. So when they tried to explain Jesus, the first Christians said simply, "Jesus is Lord."

Years ago, when I was a young Navy chaplain in the Pacific, an officer friend and I were having a discussion in my office. At one point he said abruptly, "Dick, I want to become a Christian."

His statement had come so unexpectedly that I did not know quite what to say. Naively I started to explain some of the big words I had learned in seminary, but he interrupted me. "Dick, I don't understand everything you're saying, but Jesus is my Lord. Is that enough?"

He was saying, without all the theological complexities, that he wanted to follow Jesus. Jesus was to be his leader, his master. I had sense enough to reply, "Certainly that is enough."

Some also have called Jesus Savior. He saves us from the darkness of this world or from the dark side of our own hearts. He saves us from our unproductive, sometimes evil ways.

Others have called Jesus friend. When he was here on earth, Jesus said, "Let the little children come," and they still do. Today, a five-year old boy playing cowboy with his pretend playmate, Jesus, calls out, "Come on, Jesus partner, let's ride!" Could anyone have expressed it better?

II. POWER TO BECOME

I am convinced there is a divine, friendly presence that invades not only the world but our lives. As Leslie Newbigin, a missionary for many years in India, puts it:

> Christianity, even though it is similar to other religions in some ways, is essentially different. It is not primarily opinions about God, but rather good news. The good news is that God became a man and dwelt among us so that we could see him and know him and encounter him personally.

Whatever our experience, we find Jesus when our lives turn a corner, and there he is! As Emil Brunner, the noted Swiss theologian says, we find him not in "overly intellectual approaches . . . but in personal encounter."

Or, as the Gospel of John says (1:12), "But to all who receive him, who believe in his name, he gives POWER TO BECOME children of God."

Malcolm Muggeridge was a British journalist and former editor of the English humor magazine, *Punch*. He became a world renowned TV personality and a considerable curmudgeon. In his later years, Muggeridge became an earnest follower of Jesus and wrote a book entitled *Jesus The Man Who Lives.*

In his book he writes:

I am an old man now and as I approach my end, I find Jesus' outrageous claims even more captivating and meaningful. Quite often, waking up in the night, I feel myself . . . hovering between life and death with eternity in the distance. I see my ancient carcass, prone between the sheets, stained and worn like a scrap of paper dropped in the gutter. And hovering over it, myself, like a butterfly released from its chrysalid stage and ready to fly away.

Are caterpillars told of their impending resurrection? How, in dying, they will be translated from poor earth-crawlers, into creatures of the air with exquisitely painted wings? And if told, do they believe it? I imagine the wise old caterpillars shaking their heads, "No, it cannot be; it's a fantasy."

Yet, in the limbo between living and dying, as the night clocks tick remorselessly on . . . 1 hear again the words of Jesus, "I am the resurrection and the life," and I feel myself carried along on a great tide of joy and peace.

###

CHAPTER 29

When Civilization Shifts Its Basic Outlook

THE CREATIVE, SACRIFICIAL, POWERFUL MINORITY

When terrorism dominates our security, whether it is in our country or Israel or Iraq or Spain or Russia, we begin to change our basic outlook on many things. When television influences our thought processes and computers dominate the way we act or work, when ideas of decency or corporate ethics are often violated, we begin to question long standing viewpoints.

"There is a time," Dr. Alfred Lord Whitehead has said, "when civilization is shifting its basic outlook; a major turning point in history when the presuppositions on which society is structured are being analyzed, challenged and changed."

First, let me tell you a story about a friend of mine. Nick Hood was minister of Detroit's largest black church, and he was speaking at a meeting that I attended. Unlike many stories of black people, Nick's life was not full of tragedy in the early years. Trouble came when he got to the top, after he was minister of a church with 3,000 members, after he had been elected to the city council of Detroit, even after he was respected as a leader of our nation. Then the bottom fell out.

He received a call from the Detroit Police Department informing him that his son had been arrested for pushing drugs. As Nick put it, "We had invested so many years and so many thousands of dollars on him, and our son landed in jail." Nick went on to describe the humbling experience of a father seeking clearance at the prison gate, the awkward glances from other politicians, the sleepless nights spent praying about something beyond his control. As he spoke, though, he then said the words, "God is so good to me."

There is a spiritual by that title, and even though Nick cannot sing any better than I can, pretty soon he had all of us singing, "God is so good to me."

Now, hold that story in the back of your minds, while we think about our civilization and our democracy for a moment. We have the notion that in a democracy the majority is right, or at least, the majority rules. The fact is, though, that neither of these ideas is necessarily accurate. In matters of taste, for instance, the majority often is wrong. The masses of people prefer comic books to symphony or opera or great art. THE IDEAS THAT REMAKE OUR SOCIETY ALWAYS COME FROM A MINORITY OF THE PEOPLE.

Public policy often is determined by resolute, compact, closely organized minorities who want something, then go after it. In Germany after World War I, for instance, Hitler's Brown Shirts began. Hitler even told the world what he intended to do in his book, *Mein Kampf,* "My Plan." He had a closely organized, militant minority who wanted something, and they went after it. Even in politics, it is often a self-seeking, highly organized minority that runs a city.

Jesus took this truth and put it into a story about baking bread. Here Jesus came right into the kitchen. He had often seen his mother bake bread: three measures of meal, about the right amount for a fairly large family such as Mary and Joseph had. Then knead the dough and try to hide the yeast or leaven in the dough. Hide it? Hide yeast in bread dough? Can't be done, can it? If you keep kneading, the yeast changes the dough so completely that what would have been a kind of flat cracker becomes light, fragrant hot bread! Jesus said, "The kingdom of heaven is like leaven, which a woman took and hid in three measures of meal until the whole was leavened."

Back in the time of the American Revolution, we think of all the colonists as people who put their lives, their fortunes, and their sacred honor at the disposal of the Revolution, but there is not a word of truth in it! There probably were more Tories, the people who sided with Britain, than there were revolutionists among the colonies. And, of course, there were more people who see-sawed back and forth, first on one side and then on the other, during the Revolution. They did not have strong convictions. They only hoped they were betting right on which side was going to win!

The Revolution was won, and the constitution was put in force by a compact, highly intelligent, loyal minority.

Sometimes in America, we are tempted to worship size: big cities, big buildings, and giant multi-national corporations. But size does not always indicate power. At the height of the colossal power of ancient Rome, could anyone have thought of anything smaller than the Apostle Paul in a Roman prison writing a few letters. But the result! Whoever would have dreamed that the little man with his brief epistles would become so powerful in world history?

Before and after World War II, Mahatma Ghandi confronted the British Empire on behalf of India. At that time, the empire was one of the greatest in history, and they were trying to make terms with one man who would not fight with outward weapons or use violence. Ghandi had nothing but the ideas of a minority and a quality of soul, and these ideas won Ghandi and India their freedom.

We Christians are intended to be that minority. Jesus said we are the salt of the earth, the light of the world. We are to be the leaven in the lump of humanity. There is no possible misunderstanding what Christ meant when a person becomes a real Christian. He or she is supposed to move into the small, creative, sacrificial minority that will permeate humankind with visions of a better world.

Try to think when Christianity was the most powerful: when was the Pope the head of a mighty political machine? One time, in fact, the Pope made an emperor wait three days in the snow at Canossa asking for forgiveness for something he had done. Yet, was Christianity really as powerful then as when it was composed only of small groups of men and women scattered throughout the Roman Empire presenting truths to which the future belonged?

It was then that Christians transformed life for women. In his morning prayers, for instance, a Jew thanked God that God had not made him "a Gentile, a slave, or a woman." In Greek civilization, the women lived a life of seclusion, much as many Arab women do today. Christianity transformed life for women.

It also transformed life for the weak and ill. In pagan times, the weak and ill were considered a nuisance. The first asylum for the blind was founded by Thalasius, a Christian monk. The first free medical dispensary was founded by Alopponius, a Christian merchant. The first hospital for which there is any record was founded by Fabiola, a Christian woman.

Christianity transformed life for the child. When Christianity was first beginning, divorce was so common that it was not unusual for a woman to have a new husband every year. In such circumstances, children complicated matters, and the custom of simply exposing them to death was common.

There is a letter from a man named Hilarion in Alexandria to his wife, Alis, back home. He writes, "If you bear a child, if it is a boy let it live. If it is a girl, throw it out." And Senaca, who was one of the great thinkers of Roman history, wrote, "Children who are born weak and deformed we drown."

Later, much later, Christianity captured the empire. It became wealthy and stopped challenging the world. It began compromising and defending the status quo of the world. But when was the church the most powerful?

Today my faith is not so much in the church but in the church within the church. It is a tiny minority, the spiritual leaven living and thinking above the average. Here is what I mean: in the days of slavery, there were the Simon Legrees, the below-average slaveholders who mistreated their slaves. Not every slaveholder did, of course, but the below-average Simon Legrees did. Then there were the honorable slaveholders, those who accepted slavery but cared for their slaves both physically and spiritually.

There also was a third group, both in the north and the south, who questioned the whole idea of slavery. The rules themselves were not right, they thought. The abolition of slavery depended on that minority!

Over 200 years ago in London, there were tens of thousands of homeless orphans running around the streets. A man named Robert Raikes decided to do something about it. He and a few others gathered up some of those kids on Sunday mornings and began to teach them social graces, personal hygiene and the Bible, all at the same time. They called these gatherings Sunday Schools, and that is how the Sunday School movement was born.

Many early Sunday School pupils were right out of a scene in Charles Dickens' *Oliver Twist*. They had not had an opportunity to learn to read and write because they were working in factories and living in the slums. The people who started the Sunday School movement did not just teach the Bible. They got laws passed about child labor and public education for children. They were the minority who thought the rules were wrong.

You see, we do not have to be one of the shakers and movers of our day to get things done. We excuse ourselves by thinking we are too small. Like yeast in bread?

Let's go back to that meeting I attended where Nick Hood was speaking. Another speaker was Andrew Young, former ambassador to the United Nations, former mayor of Atlanta, and also an ordained minister. Andy made a point about minority power, when he told of some recent developments with his youngest daughter. As he explained, "She has always been the unpredictable one."

While his other children were achieving academic honors, she made it a point to just get by. While the other children focused on traditional career goals, she wanted to be a dancer or an actor or a singer. While his other children pretty much did what their parents wanted them to do, she rebelled.

One evening they were talking, and she said, "Daddy, I'm going to Uganda to work with Habitat for Humanity."

Andy was shocked, because this story happened a few years ago, when Idi Amin was the erratic dictator there.

He said, "Do you realize Idi Amin has wrecked Uganda?"

"Yes ."

"Do you realize there is no real government in Uganda?"

"Yes."

"Are you aware that anybody can do anything they want to do to you in Uganda, and there is no recourse against them?"

"Yes."

"And you still want to go to Uganda?"

"I AM going to Uganda."

So, three days before he shared this story with us, Andrew Young, one of the most powerful blacks in America, stood helpless as his youngest daughter boarded a plane and flew off to

Uganda. Andy said, half in jest, "I guess I wanted her to be a respectable Christian, not a real one."

God is so good to me!

###

CHAPTeR 30

We Can't Have the Good Life All by Ourselves

"INTERDEPENDENCE IS THE MOST IMPORTANT PRINCIPLE . . ."

The foreign policy of the Kingdom of God says, "Go into all the world and preach the Gospel to every creature." We excuse ourselves saying, "We can't do that! Why, we can't possibly . . . . The whole WORLD?" Yet, Jesus said to do that, indiscriminately, whether people are good or bad, rich or poor, or worthy or good for nothing. And it was that foreign policy that kept Christianity from dying as a little sect of the Jewish faith in ancient Jerusalem. Let me explain with a story:

Ira Mead always was too busy with his corn to mingle with his neighbors. They said, "All he cares about is corn." It was true. All Ira Mead did care about in this world was corn. He spent all his time studying the soil, experimenting, even trying to create a new variety, and he succeeded. His corn took prize after prize at the state fairs. Ira Mead thought his corn proved his supremacy over the Balches and the Paxtons and everyone

211

else around there. Where Ira Mead's corn stopped and Balch corn began, big corn stopped, and runty corn began.

The next year, though, Ira made a strange discovery: corn wasn't at all like Ira Mead. Corn associated with other corn. Ira stood one day and watched the clouds of golden pollen dust blowing across his cornfield and into the Paxton's field. More than that, pollen was blowing from Fred Balch's fields into Ira's cornfield.

Ira's world began to crumble around him. One day he heard Berta's voice in one corner of the Paxton cornfield, "Just look at this ear of corn, Joe. Down near Ira's corn ours is doing just fine." That hurt Ira, because he wanted something perfect Berta couldn't have. Ira went out that night and stood in his cornfield, pondering.

The next night his wife noticed that Ira was putting corn in a basket. Ira explained to his wife, "I'm going to take some corn seed to the Balches and tell them what I know about raising corn. I cann't have good corn when their corn's poor."

People are a lot like corn. We cann't have the good life all by ourselves. We cann't have a little community of goodness and build a wall around it. We MUST go into all the world. A Massachusetts company enters a bid to buy a company in France, but it is opposed by shareholders in Bermuda. Architects from Nebraska go to Saudi Arabia to build cities for them. The computers rattle in Tokyo and affect the market on Wall Street.

Dr. Morris Fishbein of the American Medical Association says, "Starvation and epidemics do not recognize national or racial boundaries. Typhus in Russia, plague in China, dysentery in Africa, and famine in Greece may mean disaster in Italy, Japan, or the United States."

Kirtley Mather, professor of geology for many years at Harvard, speaks plainly, "Interdependence is the most important principle affecting the life of people today . . . . The earth is far better adapted for occupation by people organized on a world-wide scale than for occupation by those who insist upon building barriers between regions, or nations or even continents."

We CAN'T have the good life all by ourselves.

Martin of Tours was a Roman soldier and a Christian who lived from 317 to 397 A.D. One cold and wintry day, as he was entering a city, a beggar stopped him and asked for alms.

Martin had no money, but the beggar was cold, and Martin gave him what he had. He took off his soldier's coat, worn and frayed as it was. He cut it in two and gave half to the beggar.

That night Martin had a dream. In it he saw heaven with the angels and Jesus in the midst of them. Jesus was wearing half of the Roman soldier's cloak. One of the angels said to him, "Master why are you wearing that battered old cloak? Who gave it to you?" Jesus said softly, "My servant Martin gave it to me."

When Jesus was on earth, he told a parable of the Last Judgement, when the people of the earth are gathered before God's throne. God divides them into two groups, and he says, "Come and receive the kingdom . . . for I was hungry and you fed me, thirsty and you gave me something to drink." The good people ask, "When did we do that, Lord?" God answers, "I tell you that whatever you do for one of my poorest brothers or sisters, you do it for me."

Then the condemned say, "Lord, if we had known it was you, THEN we would have helped." The judge replies, "When you do it for one of the least, you do it for me."

We can't have the good life all by ourselves.

###

CHAPTER 31

God So Loved the Cosmos

THE CONTINUING STORY

Jesus is the hope, not only of my life but of the world. The gospel of John (3:16) expresses it, "For God so loved the world . . . ." The Greek word, which for hundreds of years has been translated "world," is cosmos, which today means an expanded world but also the universe and the whole creation. "God so loved the COSMOS that he gave his only Son . . ."

Jesus is not just an American. Jesus is universal. In fact, there was an article on art in one of our magazines recently saying that Asian artists—Chinese, Japanese, and Indian—are attempting to reclaim Jesus as being of the East, which he was. In a publication entitled *The Gospel In Chinese Art*, Jesus is drawn having the features of the Orient.

Today, non-white people are much freer in creating their own characteristics—slanted eyes, sometimes, and darker skin—in the face of Jesus. "He belongs to us," they are saying, because

Jesus is not only of western culture. Jesus is of the world, of the cosmos.

Years ago, I was a Navy chaplain in the Pacific in the last days of World War II. After the devastation of the first atom bomb in Japan, I went with an inspection team into Hiroshima. As we approached what obviously was the center of the atomic blast, we came to a small Christian church with the walls still standing. The roof had been blown off, but the walls, ever so wobbly, were upright.

I poked around in the rubble: glass fused with pieces of metal, shards of wood, and cement. As I kicked aside some of it, I found a small porcelain figure still intact. It was the figure of Jesus with a Japanese face, eyes slanted, and Oriental clothes. His arms were outstretched to the world.

Salvador Dali has painted a thoughtful rendition of Jesus on the cross, which he has entitled *Christ Of St. John Of The Cross*. It hangs in the Glasgow Art Gallery.

Instead of the emaciated figure with eyes turned skyward often painted in the Middle Ages, Dali portrays Jesus as a muscular young man hanging on the cross. He is not nailed there, however, which indicates his willingness to die. His head is bowed, and his eyes are not visible. They may be closed in prayer, or they may be looking downward at the scene below. Light is beginning to dawn, and as it spreads across the sky, it reveals the blue waters of the Sea of Galilee against the rugged and barren shoreline. There are two boats and a few fishermen preparing to begin their day on the water.

So Jesus is the Christ, not only of the heavens or the dawn or of Galilee. He is cosmic, for the world, the universe, and the whole creation.

There is a story written by Flannery O'Conner, and the main character is Mrs. Turpin (with no first name). She is a good,

Christian woman with a pesky side that does not much like the people who are not up to her standards. One day she goes to the doctor's office. While she is sitting there, she silently thanks Jesus that she is not like the others in the waiting room: ugly people, white-trash, dark-skinned people, and smelly people.

When Mrs. Turpin returns home, she goes into her backyard, gazes at the barn, and sees a vision. Reaching from the ground is a brilliant, swinging, fiery bridge raised to heaven, and along that bridge, there is a "vast horde of souls rumbling toward heaven." As O'Conner describes it, there are "whole companies of white-trash, clean for the first time in their lives. And bands of blacks in white robes, and battalions of strange, ugly people shouting and clapping and leaping."

Bringing up the end of the procession on that fiery bridge to heaven is a tribe of people whom she recognizes at once as people like herself, people who have had the good things in life. She leans closer to observe these people. They are marching behind the others with great dignity and respectable behavior. They alone are singing on key.

Mrs. Turpin can see by their shocked and altered faces that God has seen their shallow ways of doing things, which they consider virtues, and even these are being forgiven.

Isn't that what Jesus taught us? That we are not going to make it because of our own virtues? We will be with all kinds of people: blacks, yellows, reds, stupids, and shabbies. We will all be there, not because of our virtues but because . . . of . . . God's . . . great . . . grace.

A minister friend of mine said that at dinner each night he and his family all join hands and quote the words of John 3:16, "For God so loved the world that he gave his only Son, that whoever believes on him shall not perish, but have eternal life." They then raise their hands and shout, "Hurray!"

Jesus, then, is the hope, not only of my life but of your life, and he is the hope of the COSMOS.

Hurray!

###

To order additional copies of

THE CHRIST
OF EVERY ROAD

Have your credit card ready and call:

1-877-421-READ (7323)

or please visit our web site at
www.pleasantword.com

Also available at: www.amazon.com

Printed in the United States
28811LVS00001B/208-261